A Pocket Guide to College Success

Second Edition

Laramie County Community College

Jamie Shushan

**The Crimson Summer Academy
at Harvard University**

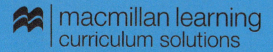
macmillan learning
curriculum solutions

bedford/st.martin's • hayden-mcneil • w.h. freeman • worth publishers

Manufactured in the United States of America.

2   1   0   9   8   7
f   e   d   c   b   a

For information, write: Macmillan Learning Curriculum Solutions, 14903 Pilot Drive, Plymouth, MI 48170 (macmillanlearning.com).

ISBN: 978-1-319-14730-3 (Laramie County Community College)

President's Welcome

LCCC Students,

I want to take a moment and personally welcome you and thank you for choosing Laramie County Community College (LCCC). You likely have landed here, now as a Golden Eagle, for a variety of reasons. Perhaps it is how affordable we are as a college, or perhaps it is one of our unique and innovative programs, or perhaps it is because you live in our communities. Regardless of the reason, you have made the right choice.

LCCC is focused on helping students transform their lives and attain their educational goal. We want—and expect—you to succeed here in your classes, when you earn your degree or certificate, and when you take that next step into your career or onto further education at one of our many university partners. While your experience here should be rewarding and memorable, it will also require commitment on your part.

That is where this course, Intro to College Success, or COLS 1000, comes in. We have designed this course to start you off right in your educational journey at LCCC. Our goals are fairly simple for this course. We want you to build positive relationships with other students and our faculty and staff. We want you to develop the skills and abilities that will make you a successful college student. We want you to decide on a program of study while exploring career options or to dig deeper into the career path you may have already chosen. Finally, we want you to learn more about you and the College as well as to realize that you have the resources and focus to succeed.

COLS 1000 is the beginning, and if you engage in this course, you will find that you will be better engaged in LCCC and better prepared for success here at the College.

If I can do anything to help you along this journey, or if you simply want to share your experience with me, my door is always open. Stop me in the halls or swing by the President's Office in the Administration Building.

I look forward to hearing about your story and, more important, shaking your hand as you walk across the stage as a graduate of Laramie County Community College!

Sincerely,

Dr. Joe Schaffer
President

LCCC 2017–2018 ACADEMIC CALENDAR

FALL 2017	Spring 2018	Summer 2018

FALL 2017

August

27 Last day to register A16 and A8

28 A16 and A8 classes begin

September

2–4 Labor Day holiday, College closed

10 Last day to register B14

11 B14 classes begin

24 Last day to register B12

25 B12 classes begin

29 Fall 2017 graduation applications due

October

20 Last day of A8 classes

22 Last day to register B8

23 B8 classes begin

31 Student and Faculty Planning Day, no classes

November

7 Spring registration begins for currently enrolled students

22–26 Thanksgiving holiday, College closed

December

15 Last day of Fall semester

23–31 Winter break, College closed

Spring 2018

January

2 College reopens

15 Equality Day, College closed

15 Last day to register A16 and A8

16 A16 and A8 classes begin

28 Last day to register B14

29 B14 classes begin

February

9 Spring graduation applications due

11 Last day to register B12

12 B12 classes begin

March

9 A8 classes end

12–18 Spring break, no classes (College services available Monday through Thursday)

16 College closed

18 Last day to register B8

19 Classes resume | B8 classes begin

April

3 Student and Faculty Planning Day, no classes

10 Summer and Fall registration begins for currently enrolled students

May

11 Spring semester ends

12 Commencement

Summer 2018

May

28 Memorial Day, College closed

28 Last day to register A10, A8, and A5

29 A10, A8, and A5 classes begin

June

1 College closed, no afternoon classes

4 Summer 2018 graduation applications due

10 Last Day to register B8

11 B8 classes begin

29 Last day of classes (A5)

July

1 Last day to register B5

2 B5 classes begin

4 Independence Day, College closed

6 Laramie Jubilee Day, Albany County campus closed

20 Last day of A8 classes

College Resources

This book serves as a guide as you start your educational journey. LCCC has many resources available to help students in their quest for success. These resources include:

- Laramie Country Community College resources;
- Albany County Campus resources; and
- Student Resources.

Take advantage of them!

LCCC Resources

The following table lists the resources that can be found on the main campus of Laramie County Community College.

- **Advising** 307-778-1214 advising@lccc.wy.edu
- **Campus Safety** 307-630-0645
- **Counseling and Campus Wellness** 307-778-4397
- **Dean of Students** 307-778-4397
- **Disability Support Services** 307-778-4397 dss@lccc.wy.edu
- **Exam Lab** 307-778-1274 examlab@lccc.wy.edu

- **Help Desk** 307-778-4357 itstech@lccc.wy.edu
- **LCCC Bookstore** 307-778-1114 bookstore@lccc.wy.edu
- **Ludden Library & Learning Commons** 307-778-1206 libref@lccc.wy.edu
- **Student Hub** 307-778-1265 studenthub@lccc.wy.edu
- **Student Success Center** 307-778-4315 tutors@lccc.wy.edu

ACC Resources

The table on the next page lists the resources that can be found on the Albany campus of Laramie County Community College.

- **ACC Bookstore**
  307-432-1667
  bookstore@lccc.wy.edu

- **ACC Test & Exam Center**
  307-772-4262
  acctesting@lccc.wy.edu

- **Advising** 307-778-1214
  advising@lccc.wy.edu

- **Albany County Campus Library**
  307-772-4263

- **Campus Safety** 307-772-4259

- **Dean of Students**
  307-772-4259

- **Disability Support Services**
  307-772-4254
  khumphrey@lccc.wy.edu

- **Help Desk** 307-778-4357
  itstech@lccc.wy.edu

- **Student Hub** 307-772-4299
  studenthublaramie@lccc.wy.edu

- **Student Success Center**
  307-772-4257
  jford@lccc.wy.edu

Student Resources

Student resources are more than simply resources. They are your friend, and like friends, they are there when you most need them. Here is what you need to know about the student resources:

EaglesEye

1. Access at https://ee.lccc.wy.edu/, or click on EaglesEye at the bottom of the LCCC homepage.

2. Log in with your username, which is in firstnamelastname format (e.g., "marysmith").

3. The temporary password will be your birth date in mmddyy format (e.g., "071383" represents a birthdate of July 13, 1983).

D2L

1. Download and install Google Chrome from google.com/chrome.

2. Access at https://lccc-wy.desire2learn.com, or click D2L at the bottom of the LCCC homepage. Also access within EaglesEye under the Student tab.

3. Log in with your username in firstnamelastname format. The temporary password is your birthdate in mmddyy format.

Free Printing and Wireless

1. Enroll at https://selfhelp.lccc.wy.edu/.
2. Your username is in firstnamelastname format.
3. The temporary password is your birthdate in mmddyy format.

Office 365 Education

1. Sign up at office.com/getOffice365.
2. Your valid school email address is firstnamelastname format.

Technology Assistance

Contact the ITS HelpDesk at 307-778-4357 or itstech@lccc.wy.edu for assistance with the instructional technology at LCCC.

Library Services

1. The Ludden Library has an extensive collection of available books and e-Books.
2. Contact the circulation desk at the library (307-778-1205) with any questions regarding how to access materials remotely, how to find quality resources, and how to correctly cite and use those resources in assignments.

LCCC Bookstore

1. Convenient search tool to locate the specific textbooks for your courses at http://laramie.textbooktech.com/.
2. 307-778-1114 or email bookstore@lccc.wy.edu

Note: This custom edition of *A Pocket Guide to College Success*, Second Edition, for Laramie County Community College omits Chapter 11, Chapter 13, Appendix A, and Appendix B, which are not covered by your instructors. As a result, you will find gaps in pagination, which are intentional.

Brief Contents

A Pocket Guide to
College Success

A Pocket Guide to College Success

Second Edition

Jamie H. Shushan

**The Crimson Summer Academy
at Harvard University**

macmillan learning
curriculum solutions

macmillan learning
curriculum solutions

bedford/st martin's • hayden-mcnell • w.h. freeman • worth publishers

bedford/st martin's • hayden-mcnell • w.h. freeman • worth publishers

For Bedford/St. Martin's

Vice President, Editorial, Macmillan Learning Humanities: Edwin Hill
Publisher for College Success: Erika Gutierrez
Senior Executive Editor for College Success: Simon Glick
Development Manager: Susan McLaughlin
Associate Editor: Bethany Gordon
Associate Production Editor: Matt Glazer
Media Producer: Sarah O'Connor
Senior Production Supervisor: Lisa McDowell
Marketing Manager: Kayti Corfield
Copy Editor: Diana Puglisi George
Indexer: Jake Kawatski
Photo Researcher: Susan Doheny
Senior Art Director: Anna Palchik
Text Design: Claire Seng-Niemoeller
Cover Design: John Callahan
Composition: Lumina
Printing and Binding: King Printing, Inc.

Manufactured in the United States of America.

2   1   0   9   8   7
f   e   d   c   b   a

For information, write: Macmillan Learning Curriculum Solutions, 14903 Pilot Drive, Plymouth, MI 48170 (macmillanlearning.com)

ISBN 978-1-319-03089-6

Acknowledgments

How to Use This Book

Stepping onto campus that first day isn't easy. But fortunately, you're not alone. You'll soon meet instructors, students, mentors, and many others to support you throughout your college experience.

You deserve to have the tools you'll need to succeed, which is why I've created this guide. It's filled with tips, strategies, and advice to help you make the most of your time in college. The guidance offered here will help make the transition easier, your academic life more manageable and engaging, and your overall college experience more fulfilling.

This is a resource for *you*. As a college student, you're in the driver's seat and will need to take advantage of the resources available on campus, to try new techniques to help you succeed in your classes, and to ask for assistance when you need it. Your goals are certainly attainable by drawing on your motivation, building resilience, working hard, and creating a strong support system.

Your fan,

Jamie H. Shushan

Jamie H. Shushan

Finding What You Need

A Pocket Guide to College Success, Second Edition, is designed to provide clear answers to your questions about what to do, where to go, and how to succeed in college. It can help you in your first year, throughout your whole college career, and in your life beyond college. In this book, you will find the tools you need to survive and thrive as you begin this new journey.

Part I, Transitioning to College, will offer you guidance and support as you adjust to college. A new Chapter 1 will help you begin to find your place in college and address academic expectations. Chapter 2 will build upon this foundation by helping you develop a college support system early on so you can ask the right questions and get the help you need. Chapter 3, also new to the second edition, will give you the tools you need to persist in college, focusing on how to maintain motivation, foster resilience, and set goals to drive your own success in college and beyond. And Chapter 4 will enable you to explore time management strategies that will keep you on track in your course work and daily life.

Part II, Study Skills, will enumerate numerous skills that are essential for your success in college. Chapters 5 through 10 focus on key study skills strategies, such as using your learning preferences to help you study; practicing five steps for critical thinking; note taking; reading effectively; focusing your energies before, during, and after test taking; and systematically building your writing and information literacy — key building blocks for academic achievement.

Part III, Skills for Success, emphasizes practical considerations that are relevant for your success in college and beyond. Chapters 12 and 14 will help you with aspects of college life beyond academics: managing money, making healthy choices, and managing stress. Lastly, Chapter 15 empowers you with concrete strategies as you begin your career exploration.

Table of Contents. Browsing through the brief table of contents at the beginning of the book will usually guide you to the information you need. If not, consult the more detailed table of contents included inside the back cover.

Getting Started Guides. Ease your transition to college by reviewing these guides at the beginning of the text to see what you should keep in mind during your first week, month, and term in college.

Index. If you can't locate what you need in either table of contents, consult the index at the back of the book, beginning on page I-1. The index can be especially useful if you're looking for something specific and you know the term for it. For example, if you want help creating a to-do list, you could simply look under "to-do list" in the index and then go to the designated pages.

Lists of Features. Just before the end of the book, you'll find a quick guide to some of the most often consulted parts of this book: "5 Questions" and "5 Ways" lists, Case Studies, Checklists, Getting Started Guides, Quick Tips, and Visual Walkthroughs (illustrated explanations of key points).

part

I

Transitioning to College

Your First Week in College

① **Gather the basics.** Pick up your student ID, set up your student e-mail account, and purchase any course materials you need for your classes such as books, pens, and notebooks.

② **Use a planner to get organized.** Figure out if you'll use paper or an electronic planner, and begin adding your class times and locations, any job hours, commute time, and other commitments including meetings, orientation sessions, family obligations, and so on.

③ **Get oriented.** Take time to familiarize yourself with campus before you need to be somewhere. Locate the buildings where your classes are held, the location of your job if you have one, places to eat, the library, the student center, the financial aid office, and so on.

④ **Focus on your living situation.** If you live on campus, unpack and begin to get settled in your new place; meet with your roommate(s) to discuss ground rules; and figure out where to eat your meals and how your meal plan works. If you commute, figure out your best mode of transportation and how much commuting time you need to allow. If you have a family, research childcare or eldercare options, if necessary.

⑤ **Introduce yourself to peers and campus staff.** Find ways to interact with your peers and strike up a conversation in your classes, during campus events and orientation, or during meals. Also, don't forget to begin reaching out to upperclassmen and campus staff when opportunities arise. Schedule an appointment with a campus staff member in your school's advising, financial aid, or career counseling office, etc., to address any questions you may have.

Your First Month in College

① **Ask questions.** Get into the habit of asking instructors, mentors, peers, upperclassmen, and campus staff any questions that arise for you.

② **Determine how you will spend your time outside of class.** Think about what else you either need or want to include in your daily and weekly routines. You may already have a job or may need to find one. You might want to schedule time for exercise or volunteering. And you'll also need to fit in any family obligations you have.

③ **Figure out when and where you will complete assignments and study for tests.** Determine when you have open blocks of time each day and where and when you are able to stay focused and get work done efficiently. Make notes of blocks of time when you are most efficient and add those as regular study times in your planner. Write down where you'll study, too.

④ **Reflect on your daily routine.** Notice what is working and what isn't about your work/life balance. Are you getting enough sleep? Are you leaving enough time to get to your classes and other obligations? How is your commute working? Are you able to fit in social activities, your family commitments, and time to relax? Be flexible and make alternative decisions on how you spend your time based on your answers to these questions.

⑤ **Assess how you're feeling about course work and take action if necessary.** Do you understand the material? If not, where are you having difficulty? Determine if you might be able to form a study group with your classmates. If necessary, meet with your instructor during office hours to discuss material and ask questions, or research your college's academic support services.

Your First Term in College

1. **Continue making connections.** Meet regularly with peers outside of class, connect with instructors during office hours, and participate in activities that are meaningful for you. Also, meet with an advisor or mentor at least once or twice during the term.

2. **Make changes to your schedule as needed.** Reflect on what worked and what didn't work, and make adjustments to your schedule to set yourself up for success in the next term. For example, if academics were harder than you expected, figure out how to fit in more study time. If you want to be more involved, you may need to investigate more deeply the activities that suit your interests and passions.

3. **Fit in activities that keep you healthy.** In your planner, write down when you plan to engage in activities you'd like to do to keep your body and mind feeling good. Maybe that means taking regular walks, meeting a friend for coffee between study sessions, or going to the gym.

4. **Get help if you need it.** College can be challenging academically, personally, and socially. There are many possible resources, such as campus support offices, peers and mentors, and counseling centers, that can offer you the support you need.

5. **Prepare for next term.** Jump into next term having learned from your first term! Reflect on what worked and didn't work academically and socially, and what you might want to change or explore as you embark on a new term and register for next term's classes. Be sure to meet any course registration deadlines and involve your instructors, mentors, and peers as you make decisions.

1

Beginning Your College Journey

A s you begin your college journey, you may feel especially eager and excited. Or you might be quite nervous about the challenges ahead. Whether this is your first time attending college or you're coming back after a break, you may have a lot of anticipation, mixed emotions, and questions as you embark on this new chapter of your life. How will college change me? What will be expected of me in my classes? Where can I find support if I need it? Give yourself time to answer these questions. And recognize that the transition to college is a big one. You will be spending your energy in significant ways as you make an enormous investment in your future. You will be asked to stretch beyond your comfort zone both personally and academically, but if you rise to meet the challenge, new opportunities can open up in your life. In addition, you'll likely have many new experiences and meet people from all walks of life. This chapter also explores how to navigate a new college culture and expectations as well as the steps you can take to begin carving out your place in college.

LaunchPad Solo
macmillan learning

To access the LearningCurve study tool, video activities, and more, go to *LaunchPad Solo for College Success.* macmillanlearning.com/collegesuccessmedia

Why Go to College?

You are likely attending college for a variety of reasons. Perhaps college feels like the logical next step after graduating from high school. Maybe you're excited to be the first in your family to go to college, or you're returning to school after a break to pursue a new career. Or maybe you don't know yet what you want to do and hope that college will help you find your passion or teach you the skills necessary to get a good job in the future. Whatever your reasons, this experience can open up new opportunities, and help you grow academically and personally.

More Opportunity

Your decision to attend college is a powerful one and something to take great pride in. Pause a moment to congratulate yourself and reflect on the path ahead. *Your* college path will be unique and distinct from the paths of those around you. The academic, social, and personal experiences that come your way will push your thinking, challenge your beliefs, and open up more opportunity for you in a number of ways.

To appreciate how your decision to go to college will likely impact your future, it's helpful to look at a number of factors. Studies have shown that higher levels of education positively affect earnings and economic growth, job status and satisfaction, health and security, and parental and civic engagement. For example, recent reports reveal that college graduates compared to high school graduates often experience the following benefits:

- Higher earnings[1]
- Lower rates of unemployment and poverty[2]

---

[1]National Center for Education Statistics, "Annual Earnings of Young Adults," ch. 1 in *The Condition of Education 2015*, May 2015, https://nces.ed.gov/programs/coe/indicator_cba.asp.

[2]Pew Research Center, "The Rising Cost of *Not* Going to College," Feb. 11, 2014, http://www.pewsocialtrends.org/2014/02/11/the-rising-cost-of-not-going-to-college/.

- More full-time job security
- Opportunity to climb socioeconomic ladder
- More satisfying career
- Health insurance benefits and pensions[3]
- Healthier lifestyles
- More volunteerism and voter participation
- Children experience more engagement and education at home

These benefits are significant when you consider the positive impact they have on your standard of living and your family's well-being, not to mention the potential community and societal benefits. Going to college is a transformative experience. It is a privilege that will help you grow in significant ways if you open up your mind to all that's possible, and work hard to make those future opportunities a reality.

Academic, Social, and Personal Growth

Opportunities for growth are abundant at college. Academically, you might be challenged by new information and explore subjects brand new to you. Socially, you may also experience growth by meeting new people from a variety of religious, ethnic, racial, socioeconomic, and political backgrounds, as well as from different parts of the country or world. And the opportunities for personal growth and development are plentiful as you take on new challenges, manage complicated schedules, and learn how to prioritize and balance work, school, and sometimes family responsibilities.

Recognize your academic opportunities. You will take many classes during college. Some will be interesting, while others may be courses you are required to take that aren't thrilling for you. Whatever the case, try to get the most out of your academic life by delving into course material in a thorough and deep way. Complete

---

[3]Baum, Sandy, Jennifer Ma, and Kathleen Payea, *Education Pays 2013: The Benefits of Higher Education for Individuals and Society*, College Board Trends in Higher Education Series, 2013, https://trends.collegeboard.org/sites/default/files/education-pays-2013-full-report.pdf.

assignments on time, study for tests, and debate class topics outside of class with your peers. When you make your academic opportunities meaningful, you will get the most out of them.

Be open to social learning. So much can be gained from exposure to new people who have completely different life stories and experiences. College could be the first time you're interacting with students, instructors, or college staff who come from a variety of backgrounds that may be very different from your own. You may feel uncomfortable with this type of difference at first if you've never experienced it before, but expanding your social life to interactions with people not like you will open your eyes to various cultures, beliefs, traditions, and ways of seeing the world that will likely enrich *your* way of seeing

"Your aptitude is very important but even more important, for success, is your attitude."

Keep a positive attitude and be open to new experiences during college. Yes, studying and academics are important, but college is about taking charge of your personal and social growth as well. Finding success in college is possible if you push yourself to try new things, face challenges with perseverance, and learn from those who have come before you.

the world. Be a listener, share your own story and background, and take time to ask questions. It's okay to disagree; just show respect as you express your own views.

Take charge of your personal growth. College can push you out of your comfort zone. College experiences are fundamental to helping you become more independent, as you have to manage new and challenging aspects of life. Whether you're beginning college for the first time, or returning to school after time away, personal development happens as you tackle a difficult class and figure out how to deal with its challenges, or determine how to balance a job with academics, volunteerism, and family responsibilities. And don't forget the challenge of budgeting and taking care of your own finances, deciding how to spend your valuable time, and making choices that could impact your future or health and well-being.

> ## ✔ Academic, Social, and Personal Growth Opportunities in College
>
> - ○ Taking courses in unfamiliar and challenging subjects
> - ○ Interacting with students from a variety of backgrounds, including different parts of the country and the world
> - ○ Learning how to prioritize and balance several responsibilities while managing a complicated schedule
> - ○ Financial decision making and budgeting
> - ○ Facing and overcoming challenges
> - ○ Pushing yourself out of your comfort zone

Navigating a New College Culture

Feeling comfortable academically, socially, and personally on campus takes time. You will find that your new college culture has specific expectations. Some expectations and aspects of this culture will be apparent right off the bat, while others won't become apparent until weeks or months later. Your job during your first year is to adjust to those new expectations and begin to carve out your place within the college culture that surrounds you. Making your college experience your own is an important part of feeling connected and invested on campus.

Meeting Expectations

In addition to academic and social expectations, you'll likely have your own personal expectations related to how you'd like to perform academically, the way you'd like to get involved on campus, and what you'll get out of the college experience. It's important to understand the expectations you are facing and to figure out how you'll manage them, along with the expectations you have for yourself.

Learn about academic expectations. Every college has certain academic expectations that are detailed in a student handbook or on an academic Web site. (See the Visual Walkthrough in this chapter.) Find out what type of grading system is used and learn how grades are calculated over the course of each term and each year so you will understand your grade point average (GPA) throughout college. Also, find out if you can take classes pass/fail (that is, classes you can take and have either "Pass" or "Fail" recorded on your transcript rather than the actual numeric or letter grade you earned). Be aware that if your course load becomes too difficult to manage or if personal circumstances get in the way, you can consider withdrawing from a course (which means officially deciding to stop taking the course in the middle of the term). Be sure to know what policies your college has in place around withdrawals.

QUICK TIP

Don't Make Course Decisions Alone

If you feel you might need to change the status of a course to pass/fail or believe it's better to withdraw completely from the course, consult with your instructor or campus staff *before* making your decision to be sure you have considered all possibilities and are getting the support you need.

Meeting academic expectations takes a lot of hard work, persistence, planning, and support, given the new challenges of college-level course work which is more rigorous than high school work. Learning about academic expectations will help you understand what grades you need to earn to stay in school, how you're expected to fulfill certain requirements, and what you need to do to complete a major or minor field of study in order to graduate. Your major field of study is the primary field you will focus on during college by taking the majority of your classes within that discipline or related disciplines and fulfilling specific class requirements; a minor is a secondary field of study, for which you will also have to fulfill specific course requirements.

QUICK TIP

Class-Specific Expectations

Each of your classes will also have its own specific academic expectations, so it is up to you to read the course syllabus (or course outline) carefully to be sure you understand what instructors expect of you. The syllabus, typically distributed on your first day of class, will outline how to do well in the course, how much each assignment and test is worth to your overall grade, and what the expectations for specific assignments might be, among other helpful information. Read your syllabus after the first class and check it frequently throughout the term. If you have any lingering questions, ask your instructor about them.

Be aware of the unwritten expectations. To do well in college, you will need to take a great deal of personal responsibility and initiative. This is expected but may not always be made explicit. For example, all students are expected to be active learners. Being an active learner means engaging with your course work in a deep way to analyze, draw connections, and apply this rigor to all aspects of class—discussions, lectures, assignments, and tests. Instructors expect students to attend class and to take responsibility for understanding the material, which means also taking the initiative to ask questions or get help if difficulty arises, and to follow up as needed. Instructors will not chase you or accept excuses if assignments are not handed in on time.

⑤ **Ways** to Use Your Course Syllabus to Meet Expectations

1.   Course Objectives

Usually the instructor outlines the general gist of what the course is about and what students will explore, discuss, and learn, giving you a good sense of what to expect in the course.

2.   Course Schedule and Instructor Office Hours

Pay attention to the course schedule that details class topics, assignments, and tests, as well as when you might be able to talk with your instructor during his or her office hours. Also check to see if there are other ways to reach out (such as via e-mail or a course Web site) during the term.

3.   Course Evaluation/Grading

Be sure you understand how you will be evaluated in the course, how much each assignment and test is worth, whether class participation will play a part in your course grade, and how much your final exam/project/paper is weighted. This will help you determine where to focus most of your time and energy in the course.

4.   Required Reading, Assignments, and Tests

Check your syllabus frequently to keep on top of any required readings, assignments, papers, problem sets, projects, lab write-ups, and tests to determine what is due each day.

5.   Course Policies and Procedures

Instructors have different rules for their classes, so check the syllabus for information on what to do in the case of a class absence, how you're able to use technology in the classroom, what happens if there is academic difficulty or misconduct, and how to request an accommodation you might need.

"Really, only you can tell yourself to giddyup."

Remember, you are in the driver's seat. Listen closely to your head and heart throughout college as you take personal responsibility for your decisions and engage actively in your learning.

Be clear about your personal expectations. You probably have a variety of personal expectations for yourself as you enter college. Some may be academic—related to how well you'd like to perform in your courses or the type of major you plan to pursue. And some may be related to how you spend your time outside of class. Write these expectations down so they can begin to form your academic and personal goals. Do you expect yourself to get a job, join certain types of activities, or try out for a sport or musical group? How do you expect you'll get involved in social offerings? Write all these expectations down because they can help you find your college niche.

CHAPTER 1

Visual Walkthrough

Academic Expectations

Colleges have academic requirements that you need to know. They are often found on an academic Web site or printed in a student handbook. It is your job to familiarize yourself with these expectations. Use the example below as a guide for what to look for, but be sure to fully understand your own college's academic expectations.

(1) Academic standards and expectations are essentially the "rules of the road,"—the general guidelines that your college has for student success and how students are expected to engage as active learners and members of a college community.

(2) An academic honor code outlines, in detail, what students must uphold in their academic lives to maintain their academic integrity and honesty. This includes refraining from cheating, plagiarizing, lying, or stealing in any way, among other expectations. Be sure to read your school's honor code carefully.

(3) The overall grading policies of an institution will vary, but essentially there will be details about how many credits or classes are necessary to graduate, what is required to graduate in a particular major, and what is needed to declare a minor or double major. There will also be information about what grades are needed to pass courses, to progress to future terms, and to be able to ultimately graduate, as well as the length of time it should take to graduate.

(4) The Student Code of Conduct is an important set of behavioral expectations that encompasses all aspects of student life on campus and outlines what happens when violations occur. Expectations may include respecting the rights of others, refraining from violence in words or actions, obeying state, federal, and municipal laws, including laws related to drinking and drug use, and so on.

①

Academic Policies

②

ACADEMIC HONOR CODE

ACADEMIC PROBATION
AND DISMISSAL

ACADEMIC STANDARDS
& EXPECTATIONS

CLASS ATTENDANCE
& ABSENCES

CLASSROOM
ATMOSPHERE

COURSE
EXAMINATIONS

③

GRADES &
GRADING POLICY

④

STUDENT CODE
OF CONDUCT

Academic Standards & Expectations

a. College is a time of fundamental growth and development, and so there is a high level of independence given to students, as they are expected to be responsible for their own learning and in charge of their learning process.

b. Given the increase in responsibility, students will spend much less time in class and are expected to spend much more time outside of class completing work, studying for tests, and reaching out for assistance as needed.

c. Students should expect material covered to be quite rigorous and fast paced, and so it is imperative that students arrive to class ready to fully participate by completing readings, assignments, and studying on time as instructed.

d. Students are expected to maintain the highest level of academic integrity and honesty when engaged in any academic endeavor, and so all work in written and spoken word must be one's own or cited properly.

e. Students are expected to maintain at least satisfactory academic progress each term to maintain their academic standing.

Q case study

Casey figures out how to face her academic challenges.

When I came to college, I was pushed much more intellectually than I had imagined I would be. The instructor for my Chemistry 101 course was clear that first day that his class would move quickly and also require that we apply chemistry concepts to novel problems we would investigate in our weekly labs. He explained that he could only cover so much during lecture, and it was up to us to be sure we understood everything in the assigned textbook as we covered each topic.

He wasn't kidding. At first I felt totally overwhelmed because I was having to spend so much out-of-class time working on assignments and studying the material. And even after all my efforts, I was disappointed by my first test grade. But then I realized it was up to me to ask more questions and get more help during office hours and at my academic support office. I had to take more personal responsibility for my own understanding, which was new for me. Once I did, my grades improved and I actually enjoyed the challenge most of the time.

QUESTIONS FOR REFLECTION   Have you felt more challenged by your classes than in high school or previous educational situations? Be specific about what is most challenging. Is it the actual material, the volume of reading, paper writing, test taking, or something else? Once you determine the specific ways you are feeling challenged, talk to your instructor or an academic support counselor to find out strategies to help you manage the challenges you are facing.

Finding Your Place in College

There are lots of choices you'll have in college, and many decisions you'll need to make. As you decide what you'll study and how you'll spend your time outside of academics, you'll be finding your place in college. This will probably evolve over time as the decisions you make and the experiences you have teach you more about yourself. You may even be inspired to make different choices or to try out new experiences.

Your academic focus may not be what you expect. If you know what you want to study, that's great. If you don't know what you want to study, that's totally fine, too. Just remember that when you're actually in classes, and learning material, you may end up going a different direction from the one you expected for yourself. In other words, you may really like a subject you never expected or discover that what you thought you wanted to study isn't for you. Whatever happens, prepare to be flexible. You might decide to look into other academic areas that may be a better fit.

Develop a social circle. There are lots of ways to be social and meet new people during college. Social activity can develop out of participating in a campus organization or event, forming study groups, or getting involved through volunteering or a job. The key is to find social connections that you enjoy outside of your classes. You'll likely encounter many types of social experiences during your first few months of college, and then figure out where you're most comfortable. You'll also likely learn the right balance between having a social life and keeping on top of your academics. This process may take some time. Don't worry! Keep pushing to find the social life that feels right to you. It's time well spent so that you are honoring who you are and what you want to do.

QUICK TIP

Check In with Yourself

Meeting new people and engaging in social activities can be fun, but it can also be a source of stress. And if you are a commuter student or work full time, you might be frustrated because you can't engage in social life as much as you may want to. Striking a balance is key. During your first few months of college, make sure that you are making enough time for unwinding and relaxing.

Spend your time in ways that work for you. Your personal time outside of academic classes and studying is precious. And while there will be other obligations that fill much of your time, such as a job or family needs, there is usually some personal time left over. Be deliberate about how you spend that time. You might pursue a passion in music, volunteer, or choose to spend time with your family. You might leave time to read for pleasure or watch your favorite shows. It's your time, and if you spend that time, even if it's limited, doing things that are meaningful to you, you're helping yourself to find a balance that works.

5 Questions to Help You Find Your Place in College

1. What are my academic interests?

Finding your academic place is essential. You'll be spending a lot of time engaged in academic work, so take the time to explore different subjects as fully as you can to determine what suits you.

2. What activities, clubs, organizations, or sports do I want to engage in?

Some schools host an informational fair where clubs and organizations share what they do so that new students can determine what they'd like to join. You can also check out your college's Web site to see what you can get involved with either on or off campus. Whether you're interested in writing for a school newspaper, joining a cultural organization, volunteering, or connecting with other commuter students, there will likely be many options to choose from.

3. What do I want my social life to look like?

Connecting with other people is an important part of your college experience. Often there are college-sponsored social events that happen on campus throughout the year, and you may also be in or near a town or city with opportunities to explore cultural or musical venues. If you are a commuter student, make an effort to connect with classmates outside of class. Schedule time to get coffee in town or go to a movie together over the weekend.

4. What health priorities do I have?

Determine if there are things you want to incorporate in your life that involve health and wellness because choices you make could help you meet others who have similar interests. For example, if you plan to make exercise a weekly priority, maybe there is a gym class or sports team you could sign up for. Or if healthy cooking is a passion, see if there's a cooking club you could join or you might make connections by inspiring others to help you in the kitchen.

5. How can I step out of my comfort zone?

Maybe you're excited to try something new on campus. What is it and how can you try it out? If you like it, how can you make it part of your regular routine?

2

iStock.com/CargriOgner

Finding Support on Campus

Y ou're never alone at college. Classmates jam lecture halls, students and faculty pass each other on campus, and herds wait in line for lunch in the food court. But you may still feel pangs of loneliness, even with this hustle and bustle. You might even feel isolated or afraid, especially during your first year. These feelings are completely normal. You're probably in unfamiliar territory, with new faces, new rules, and new experiences. But when you enter college, you'll have access to a wide range of support and resources that you can call upon when you need guidance or help. It's your job during your first year of college to begin seeking out those connections and support. Developing authentic relationships does take time, but it is important to start making connections with your peers, faculty, and staff on campus and to begin building a system of support that you'll be able to rely on throughout your undergraduate experience.

LaunchPad Solo
macmillan learning

To access the LearningCurve study tool, video activities, and more, go to *LaunchPad Solo for College Success.* macmillanlearning.com/collegesuccessmedia

Begin Creating a College Network

Creating a college network is crucial. The more people you meet early on in your college career, the more support you can build for yourself and the more likely it is that you'll find a few people to whom you feel particularly connected and whom you can trust. These people become your mentors: experienced and trusted persons whom you can reach out to for advice and guidance. Your peers will become very important people for you during and after college and can serve as mentors and sources of support as you navigate the transition to college. Colleges also have several resources and offices that you can tap into for additional guidance. When these resources on campus serve as sources of encouragement for you, it becomes easier to navigate the sometimes overwhelming transition to college. Let's explore three of the most powerful ways you can begin making connections on campus: finding a mentor, meeting peers, and getting to know campus offices.

Mentors Are Invaluable Resources

Mentors can come in all sorts of forms. A mentor might be an instructor you have worked with closely in the classroom, your boss, a coach you see regularly, a peer, or a college staff member you interact with frequently. During your first year, try to get to know at least one person on campus well enough to consider him or her your mentor. This relationship is invaluable because mentors are invested in your well-being and want to offer assistance when they can.

Seek out your mentor regularly. Talk to your mentor when you need advice or support or when you just want to share an exciting life development. Be honest about both your triumphs and your struggles. The more you develop this relationship and practice honest communication, the more your mentor can serve as an advocate and a wise counsel as you deal with the regular ups and downs of college.

Share your academic history. Sharing your academic history, including any past struggles you've had, will improve how your

© Fran/CartoonStock.com

College can be a confusing place sometimes. Mentors provide you with the map to navigate the maze of college and can help you feel more confident in your decisions and path forward.

mentor can advise you. For example, if you have always suffered from test anxiety, your mentor may be able to suggest appropriate academic resources to assist you. If you are a returning student, consider sharing your previous college experience and why you decided to take time off and then return.

Nourish mentoring relationships over the long term. Keep your mentor updated on how you're doing throughout college. He or she will be interested in being a part of your growth academically and personally. By staying in touch with your mentor, your level of comfort will continue to increase, sustaining an essential part of your support network.

Make Connections with Peers

Some of the most important people you will meet in college will be your peers. Peers and other students, both young and old, can be an invaluable source of strength as they are (or were) in the same boat and can relate to what you are going through, sometimes more directly than a mentor can. Start making connections with your peers during and outside of class. Some peer connections will be easy to make and others will take more time. But you will be grateful you made an effort to connect. And here's why.

Peers provide real-time support. Connecting with peers can occur in many places and at all times of the day and night—during a class discussion, in a study group, in a student activity or organization, while commuting, or at a meal. Start by introducing yourself, asking questions, and sharing aspects of yourself to truly connect. You'll find that the peer connections you begin making become essential. For example, becoming acquainted with the people around you who are going through similar experiences will enable you to discuss the challenges you share and find ways to manage them. Often the relationships formed during college last far into the future and become supportive lifelong friendships.

QUICK TIP

Be Vulnerable

Being vulnerable and talking about what is really going on in your life with others can open up room for an even bigger connection to develop. This helps others get to know you and makes it easier for them to provide any support you might need throughout college.

Experienced students have advice to offer. Connecting with experienced students is another way to find support because they often have helpful suggestions based on their college experiences. For example, they might offer ideas about what classes to take, how to manage assignments in certain disciplines, where to get help on campus, or the best places to eat in town. Some schools connect new students with peer mentors who are experienced students interested in helping new students acclimate by offering advice about academics, social life, and everything in between. If this type of peer mentoring isn't an option, try to connect with experienced students in your classes, in the organizations you join, or among your coworkers at your job.

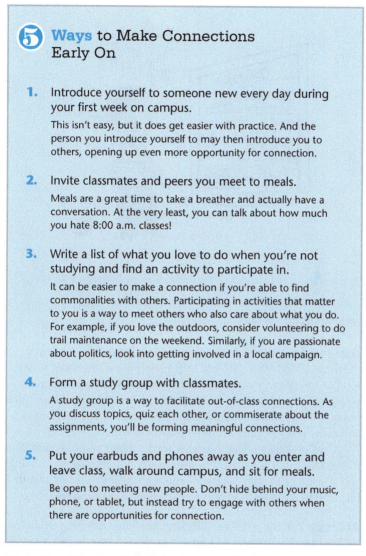

(5) Ways to Make Connections Early On

1. Introduce yourself to someone new every day during your first week on campus.

This isn't easy, but it does get easier with practice. And the person you introduce yourself to may then introduce you to others, opening up even more opportunity for connection.

2. Invite classmates and peers you meet to meals.

Meals are a great time to take a breather and actually have a conversation. At the very least, you can talk about how much you hate 8:00 a.m. classes!

3. Write a list of what you love to do when you're not studying and find an activity to participate in.

It can be easier to make a connection if you're able to find commonalities with others. Participating in activities that matter to you is a way to meet others who also care about what you do. For example, if you love the outdoors, consider volunteering to do trail maintenance on the weekend. Similarly, if you are passionate about politics, look into getting involved in a local campaign.

4. Form a study group with classmates.

A study group is a way to facilitate out-of-class connections. As you discuss topics, quiz each other, or commiserate about the assignments, you'll be forming meaningful connections.

5. Put your earbuds and phones away as you enter and leave class, walk around campus, and sit for meals.

Be open to meeting new people. Don't hide behind your music, phone, or tablet, but instead try to engage with others when there are opportunities for connection.

Campus Staff Want to Connect

In addition to peers, there are a number of offices on campus that are focused on assisting college students with various aspects of

© Andrew Toos/CartoonStock.com

Whether your campus is large and complex or relatively small and accessible, it takes time to figure out how to find all the resources at your college. Give yourself that time, be patient, and reach out to the many campus supports available to you.

their lives. You might be able to connect with a staff member in the financial aid office who can help answer questions about your scholarship or connect with an advisor or counselor you can meet with regularly throughout the term. Mentor relationships often come out of these connections. And finding a mentor or two on campus will make you feel more at home and supported.

Many of these student resources are described in this section. The names of the offices will vary by institution, and the resource offerings will also not be the same at every school, so during your first month on campus, try to learn what types of resources your college offers.

Academic Advising Office. Find the Academic Advising Office (or equivalent office) at your college and schedule a meeting with a staff member who can help you choose classes, discuss academic planning, and answer other academic questions you might have.

First-Year Programs Office. Staff members in the First-Year Programs Office are focused solely on the experience of first-year students, so stop by and find out if a staff member can assist you.

Specific academic departments. If you have questions about specific classes and the requirements for particular majors, meet with a departmental advisor in that particular field of study (for example, biology, psychology, or English).

 # case study

Lisa, in her first term of college, dealt with a challenging advising situation. But after advocating for herself, she managed to turn the situation around. Here is her story.

An advisor I first connected with at college was not very helpful. When I tried reaching him for additional academic advice after I set up our first meeting, he was never available. He wasn't very personable, and that intimidated me. I didn't get the support I needed, and the lack of support discouraged me from seeking more help. I talked with a few other students I trusted, who suggested that I visit the First-Year Programs Office. I finally decided that things weren't going to change unless I took some initiative, so after class one day I stopped by the First-Year Programs Office. A staff member in the office took the time to meet with me, and we hit it off. I asked her if we could stay in touch throughout the semester, and she happily agreed. My new contact was welcoming, encouraging, and realistic, qualities I needed as an insecure first-year student. When I had questions, she would direct me to the right person or would try to point me in the right direction. She was my main academic support until I declared my major and found an advisor in the International Relations Department. However, she became my mentor, and I continued to meet with her often.

QUESTIONS FOR REFLECTION   Does Lisa's story resonate with your advising experience? Have you received the advising that you need to feel supported? Do you know of any other advising resources you should tap into?

Academic Support and Tutoring Office. If you find yourself struggling in a class, check out the services at your college's Academic Support and Tutoring Office. Whether you're having difficulty with the reading load, experiencing trouble studying and remembering information, or receiving low grades on quizzes and tests, take advantage of all that your college offers, including tutoring. Colleges can usually find tutors in any subject area or at the very least will determine what resources are available to help you.

Writing and math centers. Your college campus might have other key academic resources, such as a writing center and a math center. Determine what these centers offer and when they're open. Use the writing center if you need help with an assigned paper—even if you think it's well written—or if you are struggling with written exams. Use the math center to help you complete homework assignments, understand important concepts, or practice finishing tests in the time allotted. Each of these centers offers one-on-one help and serves as a place to study so that you have immediate access to assistance if you run into difficulty.

Counseling centers. Many campuses have various counseling offices dedicated to supporting students with any challenges they might face during college, including academic struggles, personal issues, and social dilemmas. You might seek assistance from a counselor if you're experiencing test anxiety, constantly feel overwhelmed, have medical problems, or are dealing with relationship or family difficulties. During college, it's normal to experience tough times that require more than friendly advice from a peer. College counselors understand students' struggles and can offer needed support.

Financial Aid Office. During your first few weeks on campus, introduce yourself to your financial aid officer. Financial issues or questions can arise at any time, so having a connection in the Financial Aid Office is a great advantage. The conversations you have with him or her will demystify the financial aid process, making it easier when you apply for financial aid throughout your college years.

Career Services Office. The sooner you find your way to the Career Services Office, the sooner you'll discover the many resources this office provides, including career advice, assistance with summer jobs, and counseling to help you determine which classes and majors are appropriate for you.

Student Employment Office. If you need to work during college, visit your Student Employment Office in person or check out its Web site for job postings. This resource can help you find work both on and around campus, and includes regular employment opportunities as well as work-study jobs. Sometimes this office is a part of the Financial Aid Office.

Student Services Center. To learn how to get involved in campus activities, visit the Student Services Center (or equivalent office), where you can meet with staff who oversee campus activities and clubs. Determine how you'd like to connect with your peers through your college's various options. Building a connection to campus beyond the classroom will help you feel supported and more at home.

The library. Not only does the library offer books, journals, and online resources, but it also provides many supportive services for students. Librarians have research expertise that you can draw on, and they will help you find the information you need for assignments. Also available are computer and printing services.

Disability Services Office. If you need disability services of any kind, be sure to seek support from your campus Disability Services Office. Staff members will determine how best to assist you.

Diversity centers. Campus diversity centers provide a space for students of different ethnic, religious, or cultural backgrounds to come together in a variety of ways. You will find opportunities to organize multicultural events, join clubs, participate in discussions, meet with center staff members, or enjoy a place to study and socialize.

The offices described above are staffed with people who want to support students through their college experience. Use these valuable resources whenever and as often as you need them.

CHAPTER 2

Visual Walkthrough

Find Campus Resources Online

During the first few weeks on campus, take time to explore the various links on your college's Web site. Campus resources—such as academic support, counseling services, financial aid, and student employment and career services—usually have their own pages. And the college's Web site often lists club and athletic-related information, on-campus events, transportation schedules, and town/city happenings. Remember, resources are unique to each institution, so those detailed below are only examples. Checking your college's Web site is the best way to find out what resources you will find on campus.

(1) Use this academic support office for one-on-one help whenever you are experiencing academic challenges in your courses.

(2) Find answers to financial aid questions, meet with officers when you have concerns, learn more about your aid package, and access forms you need to fill out each year.

(3) Search for employment opportunities of all types, including work-study positions and sometimes jobs that are off campus, but close by.

(4) Download bus schedules on your device so that you're not late to class or work if you're commuting or if your dorm is a long distance from academic buildings.

(5) Check out this page if you're interested in participating in campus sports or recreational activities and want to learn about ways to stay healthy and fit.

(6) Visit for advice and information about careers, summer internships, résumé writing, job applications, and more; take advantage of advising services to help determine what classes and majors are appropriate for you.

(7) Learn about the many opportunities to meet and find support from students and staff from diverse backgrounds, including mentoring, social events, clubs and organizations, cultural enrichment, and academic assistance.

Current Students

Make the most of your UMass Amherst education by embracing all the opportunities, resources, and the diversity of our campus. Take advantage of the broad range of academic programs and the Five College Interchange. Consider co-curricular options, internships and co-ops, and study abroad to lay the foundation for a rewarding career. Rely on our network of campus support services to provide key assistance as you work steadily toward your goals.

Academic Resources

- Academic Advising
- Community Service Learning
- Five College Interchange
- General Education Program (Gen Ed)
- Graduate Programs and Degrees
- Graduate Student Handbook
- Graduation Information
- Learning Commons
- Libraries
- Office of Undergraduate Research and Studies
- Registrar
- Study Abroad
- Tutoring and Supplemental Instruction

Daily Life

- Bookstore
- Bus Schedules and Maps
- Campus Recreation and Sports Clubs
- Center for Student Development
- Dean of Students
- Dining on Campus
- Family Housing
- Fraternities and Sororities
- Health Services
- Personal Safety
- Registered Student Organizations
- Residential and Spiritual Life
- Student Government Association
- Student Success Centers

Financial Services

- Bursar's Office (Bill Payment)
- Financial Aid Services
- Graduate Assistantships
- Scholarships
- Student Employment

Services and Resources

- Career Services
- Counseling and Psychological Health
- Diversity Matters
- Everywoman's Center
- Graduate Employee Organization
- Multicultural Programs and Services

University of Massachusetts, Amherst

> ## ✓ Campus Resources Checklist
>
> Locate and visit the following campus resources, as applicable to your school, on campus or online:
>
> - ○ Academic Advising Office
> - ○ First-Year Programs Office
> - ○ Specific academic departments
> - ○ Academic Support and Tutoring Office
> - ○ Writing and math centers
> - ○ Counseling centers
> - ○ Financial Aid Office
> - ○ Career Services Office
> - ○ Student Employment Office
> - ○ Student Services Center
> - ○ Library
> - ○ Disability Services Office
> - ○ Diversity centers

Instructors Are Part of Your Network, Too

When considering the numerous ways you can seek support during college through mentors, peers, and the many student support offices on campus, don't forget the support you'll receive by visiting your instructors after class or during their office hours. Don't rely on e-mail as your only means of communication. Take the time to talk with your instructors so that they understand who you are as a student, beyond your test scores and graded assignments. Show your instructors your interest in the courses they teach, and ask them thoughtful questions so that they can see the effort you're putting into studying the course material. Spend time getting their advice about papers and studying, and discuss aspects of the course that you don't understand. Getting to know your instructors can help you in your college career, especially if you are struggling in some way.

Make the Most of Office Hours

The first week of class, instructors usually post their office hours—the hours during the week when they are available to meet with students. Visiting an instructor during office hours is a great way to meet privately with him or her to introduce yourself, discuss interesting aspects of the class, share your progress on a paper, talk about your grade on the last quiz, or ask for studying and test-taking advice. Talking privately with your instructor might feel a bit daunting, but these meetings can make a big difference in helping you understand the material and thus improve your ultimate performance in the course. Be sure to spend five to ten minutes preparing for the meeting by writing down what you plan to ask so that you make the most of your time.

---

⑤ Questions to Ask Your Instructor during Office Hours

1. I'm still struggling to fully understand this concept. Are there additional examples, evidence, or an experiment you could share with me that illustrates this particular class concept?

When you are confused, be specific about what you don't understand and think about what it is that might aid your understanding.

2. Could we debate this topic out loud so I can test my paper argument?

Engaging in a discussion about your paper will open up opportunities for more critical thinking as you weigh the pros and cons of your argument with an expert in the field.

(continued)

(continued)

3. **Do you have any study strategies that you think work particularly well for this type of material?**

    Your instructor may have course-specific study strategies that can help you learn the material more deeply, engage with the material more critically, and retain the material more easily.

4. **Can we go over what types of analysis and explanations you were looking for on this question so I have a better idea for our next exam?**

    Look over what you got wrong on past tests with your instructor and find out what you could do differently or more thoroughly on future tests to improve your success.

5. **Is there any additional research, reading, or video material I can look at? Any hands-on experiences I can engage in, or any experiments I could do to broaden my perspective on this topic?**

    Find out if there are supplemental activities you could undertake to improve your learning and interest in the class.

Share Your Academic Struggles

The academic rigor of college courses usually surpasses that of high school courses. Therefore, most students face real challenges in college-level classes. And while you adjust to college academics, you might not earn the grades you did in high school. If you find yourself struggling with course material at any point during the term, meet with your instructors after class or during office hours. They will see your effort and your desire to succeed, even if your grades don't seem to match, and they will try to help you in whatever ways they can.

QUICK TIP

Identify the Problem

Are you studying a new subject? Do you have test-taking anxiety? Do you need a new study strategy? By assessing the root of your academic challenges, you can identify how to overcome them.

Ask Questions and Get Help Often

Let's face it. The transition to college is hard. Sometimes you might still feel uncertain, overwhelmed, and alone even when you are surrounded by a supportive network. Even though it may seem that everyone else knows what to do, where to go, what classes to pick, how to study, what extracurricular activities to join, and how to balance academics with a job, many students hide their real fears, academic struggles, and confusion. In fact, most students, especially during their first year, experience anxiety, but few are willing to be honest about it.

Anxiety Is Understandable

Walking into a college world that is different from what you are used to can be scary, especially if everything is new to you. If you have a family, you may be nervous about how attending school will affect your partner or children; if you are a returning student, you may be nervous about resuming your education after a long time away from academic life. Whatever your background, you will need to pick classes, often without knowing what you will major in, and you will constantly be faced with important decisions: Is this activity worth my time? What requirements should I fulfill this term? How many hours a week should I be studying and working? Dealing with all the newness and decision making can be very jarring, especially because you may feel like you're the only one who doesn't fit in. However, it's perfectly normal if you find it challenging to manage certain aspects of your new college life. Fortunately, you don't have to manage them alone.

Seeking Assistance Is Key

Reach out to the college's many resources if you need help for any reason—academic or personal. Too many college students pretend that they don't need help with their course work when in fact they are struggling. Or they try to dismiss difficult personal, familial, or social pressures that continue to build. These students are fooling themselves and will only suffer as a result. Acknowledging that college may be challenging for you is the first step toward facing your fears and persevering. Success in college requires the courage to ask questions all the time and to get help as soon as you need it. In college, you are surrounded by an extensive support network—peers, mentors, instructors, friends, and family—all rooting for you to succeed. But you need to tap into those resources.

Getting help in college is a courageous act. It's also an essential life skill. In any job or relationship, being able to ask questions and reach out for help leads to successful careers and fulfilling lives. We all experience fear and struggles, but being able to find the right support helps get us through difficult times.

3

Motivation and
Goal Setting

In college, you'll likely face balancing challenges every day, from academics with a job to studying for a difficult exam to taking care of a sick family member. College offers many exciting opportunities, but you will likely also face obstacles. However, strategies and habits of mind, such as mindset, resilience, and grit, can help you persevere. By determining which motivators play a role in your life, as well as how the way you see the world impacts your decisions and actions, you'll be better able to manage what comes your way.

Similarly, setting goals will allow you to align yourself with your purpose for being in college. Essentially, goals are your road map to success in all areas of your life. The more meaningful your goals are, the more motivated you'll feel. And when you combine your motivation with an ability to adapt to setbacks and challenges, you'll be able to perform at your best and sustain the effort required to accomplish your goals.

LaunchPad Solo
macmillan learning

To access the LearningCurve study tool, video activities, and more, go to *LaunchPad Solo for College Success*. macmillanlearning.com/collegesuccessmedia

Motivation Matters

If this is the first time you're thinking deeply about motivation, you might ask yourself why it is so important. Whether you realize it or not, motivators affect our decisions and actions every day. And as you take on new responsibilities and independence in college, learning about what motivates you matters greatly. Your motivation determines how committed you'll be to your course work and how you'll overcome obstacles in achieving your goals.

Types of Motivation

There are two basic categories of motivation to be aware of: extrinsic and intrinsic.

Extrinsic motivators come from other people and the external world. This type of motivation stems from the promise of an external reward or fear of an undesirable outcome. Perhaps you are in school to learn new skills so that you can get a promotion at work. Or maybe you are committed to maintaining a certain GPA in order to keep your scholarship or transfer to another college. These are examples of external forces pushing you to pursue certain goals.

Intrinsic motivators come from your personal interests, desires, and standards. This type of motivation derives from your internal desire to achieve. For example, you may love math because you get a great deal of personal satisfaction out of working through a problem

---

QUICK TIP

The Power of Intrinsic Motivation
Depending on the situation, both extrinsic and intrinsic motivation are influential and can help you reach your goals. However, intrinsic motivation can be more powerful. Why? Because when you are accomplishing goals for your own satisfaction rather than for others, the achievement is often more meaningful.

in order to get to the right answer. This internal sense of fulfillment propels you to work hard and push through challenges because you feel a sense of accomplishment when you solve the problem. When intrinsic motivators are at play, the decisions you make and actions you take feel quite personal because *your* thinking and reasoning are the driving forces.

"I owe my success to my mother, who egged me on."

© Martha Campbell/CartoonStock.com

Sometimes an important family member, such as your mother, can serve as a powerful extrinsic motivator. However, both intrinsic and extrinsic motivators will play a role in your success in college. What are some motivators that push you to succeed?

What Motivates You Academically?

Let's dig into what motivates *your* actions and decisions. Think about what prompts you to read a book, go to class, or complete a work project. This can help you understand yourself better and make college decisions that work for you. To get at both extrinsic and intrinsic motivators, consider specific aspects of your academic life and think deeply about how motivation plays into your decisions and actions (see the 5 Questions List).

With your academic motivators in mind, assess which ones are the most powerful for you and write them down. Reminding yourself what is at the core of what motivates you will help you take actions that will be personally fulfilling and will keep you moving forward—even during tough times.

---

⑤ Questions to Help You Understand Your Academic Motivators

1. What motivated me to apply and attend college?

Think about factors that influenced your college application process and why you decided to enroll at your college.

2. What motivates me to pay attention in class?

Think about when you are most likely to stay focused during a lecture or want to participate in a class discussion.

3. What motivates me to complete assignments and study for tests?

Consider the times you find it easiest to get started on your work without procrastination.

4. What motivates me to keep working when I am challenged or struggling in a class?

Think about how you have overcome academic challenges and what you have done when you've struggled with academic work.

5. What motivates me to work hard in a class?

Consider the moments in your academic life where you pushed yourself to work to the best of your ability.

Mindset, Resilience, and Grit Matter, Too

As we've seen in the last section, understanding what motivates you in your academic life provides important insights into how you can succeed in college. And it turns out that your mindset, or the way you see yourself and experience the world, also matters when it comes to college achievement. Having the right mindset can impact the decisions you make, your actions, and the way you deal with challenges along the way. Similarly, traits such as resilience and grit, which refer to your ability to bounce back from disappointments and setbacks, also make an impact on your success in college.

Understanding Your Mindset

After years of research focused on achievement and success, Stanford University psychologist Carol S. Dweck found that there are two mindsets that can exist for an individual: a growth mindset or a fixed mindset. Each affects achievement and success in different ways.

Learn the difference between a growth mindset and a fixed mindset. People with a growth mindset believe that traits like intelligence and personality are not set in stone, but instead are able to change and develop.[1] If you have a growth mindset, you tend to see challenges as an opportunity for growth, push yourself to try new things, and learn from your mistakes and criticism.

In contrast, those with a fixed mindset tend to believe people are born with qualities, like a set level of intelligence or a certain personality, that are unchangeable over time.[2] Overcoming challenges can be harder if you have a fixed mindset because you can view failure as a sign that you don't have the ability to achieve a particular task. For example, upon receiving a poor grade on a paper, a student with a fixed mindset would assume that he or she is bad at writing. However, a student with a growth mindset would view the criticism as constructive and seek to improve on the next paper.

---

[1]Dweck, Carol S., *Mindset: The New Psychology of Success*, Ballantine Books, New York, 2006, 5.

[2]Ibid., 6.

QUICK TIP

Be Honest with Yourself

Sometimes people can have different mindsets about different tasks. For example, you may find that you have a growth mindset about your creative pursuits, but a fixed mindset about completing your math homework. Reflect on what might have caused your mindsets. Did you have a negative experience involving a particular subject? Did a supportive teacher help you excel at a specific topic? Does a task simply not appeal to your interests? Wherever you are right now, it's okay. Being honest with yourself is the first step in shifting your mindset.

Developing a growth mindset in college. A growth mindset is crucial so that you can pick yourself back up and learn from any experiences that fall short of your expectations. Here are a few tips on how to develop a growth mindset:

- Consider what intrinsically motivates you to persevere academically, even in the face of obstacles. What do you want to achieve in college? What could help push you to persist? Whatever the answers are, remind yourself of them when you are feeling challenged.

- Acknowledge when you are challenged and when you are frustrated. College-level work is inherently difficult, and most college students face many academic challenges. Whenever you feel that way, you are certainly not alone. Talk to a peer, mentor, or instructor you trust and share your difficulties.

- When you struggle or your efforts aren't producing successful results, take a break. Then, step back and figure out what might be going on and enlist the perspective of someone in your college support system. Do you need additional help in the class? Do you need to learn new college study strategies? Do you need to put in more time outside of class? Focus on what you *can* do to move yourself forward, rather than on whether you are lacking in some way.

Q case study

Mindset Makes a Difference

Andrew explains how he dealt with failure during his first month on campus.

I was shocked to get my first English paper back with a grade of C-. I'd never gotten below a B on a paper in my life, and I had spent countless hours writing the paper and even pulled an all-nighter before it was due. I felt incredibly frustrated and discouraged after class. After sharing the news with one of my classmates who also didn't do well on the paper, I felt a bit better, and remembered that my high school hadn't done all that much to prepare me for college-level writing. In fact, the college English paper was the longest paper I'd ever written that required using multiple sources. And I also hadn't asked for any feedback on my paper outline. I knew this was just one of many papers I would have to write and the sooner I figured out how to improve, the better off I'd be.

I decided to meet with my instructor about my paper. After speaking with my instructor, I learned my ideas were good, but my organization and logic needed more work. She suggested working on the next paper well in advance of the due date and to take advantage of her office hours for initial feedback—and the college's Writing Center staff as well. I was determined to improve and found that my next paper, while still difficult, felt less daunting since I gave myself time to get necessary feedback I could incorporate.

QUESTIONS FOR REFLECTION   What happens to you when you don't succeed in the ways you expect? Who could you talk to at your college when you struggle and need to figure out how to manage an academic challenge? Can you think of one or two things you could do to proactively help yourself overcome academic obstacles?

Resilience, Grit, and Achievement

Motivation requires a lot of courage and persistence. It also takes resilience, or the ability to bounce back after experiencing setbacks in life, and grit, which consists of determination and a sustained effort to work toward long-term goals despite unexpected struggles and slow progress.[3] Given the many bumps and obstacles that will present themselves along the path to a college degree, resilience and grit, combined with a growth mindset, will help you persist.

Becoming a more resilient and gritty person involves shifting your perspective and viewing failure as an opportunity for learning rather than a reflection of personal fault. Additionally, having the ability to control your emotions, and change course when necessary is an important quality of resilient students. College is a long-term

" My ability to adapt is the key to my success. "

© Roy Delgado/CartoonStock.com

Being able to adapt to new situations is a critical skill that you will use throughout college and the rest of your life. Be sure to employ the strategies described in this chapter to cultivate a growth mindset and become more resilient and gritty.

---

[3]Duckworth, Angela, et al., "Grit: Perseverance and Passion for Long-Term Goals," *Journal of Personality and Social Psychology*, vol. 92, no. 6 (2007): 1087–1101.

endeavor that takes stamina, interest, and vision. Becoming more resilient and gritty is certainly beneficial when it comes to college achievement and achieving goals—a topic we'll explore in more detail in the next section.

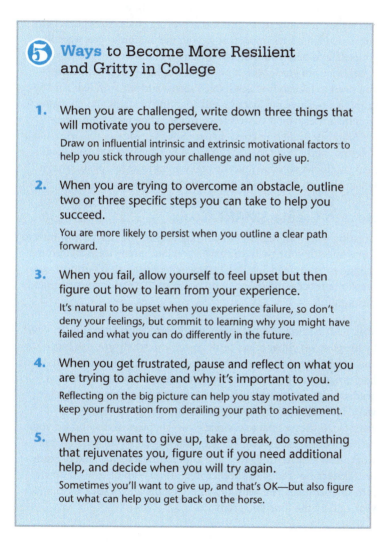

⑤ **Ways** to Become More Resilient and Gritty in College

1. When you are challenged, write down three things that will motivate you to persevere.

Draw on influential intrinsic and extrinsic motivational factors to help you stick through your challenge and not give up.

2. When you are trying to overcome an obstacle, outline two or three specific steps you can take to help you succeed.

You are more likely to persist when you outline a clear path forward.

3. When you fail, allow yourself to feel upset but then figure out how to learn from your experience.

It's natural to be upset when you experience failure, so don't deny your feelings, but commit to learning why you might have failed and what you can do differently in the future.

4. When you get frustrated, pause and reflect on what you are trying to achieve and why it's important to you.

Reflecting on the big picture can help you stay motivated and keep your frustration from derailing your path to achievement.

5. When you want to give up, take a break, do something that rejuvenates you, figure out if you need additional help, and decide when you will try again.

Sometimes you'll want to give up, and that's OK—but also figure out what can help you get back on the horse.

Set SMART Goals

Your motivation and mindset will not only help you manage challenges, excel, and achieve in college, but they are also useful tools when it comes to setting and achieving goals. Your goals help you articulate what's important to you, the outcomes you want for yourself, and why you want to work hard and succeed. They provide a path that can guide you in powerful ways by laying out the steps you need to take to find academic success and feel fulfilled. And by keeping a positive perspective and adapting to stress and changing circumstances, you'll stay on track toward achieving those goals.

Start out by setting goals that are Specific, Measurable, Attainable, Relevant, and Timely, or "SMART."[4] Why? Because SMART goals help you focus on what it is you really want to accomplish, what it will take to get there, and how you'll know if you are on track.

How to Create SMART Goals

Creating goals can feel overwhelming. Maybe you don't know how to come up with your goals, or maybe you have many ideas swimming around in your head, but don't know where to start. It's important to break the process of goal creation down so that it is manageable and meaningful.

Step 1: Differentiate between short- and long-term goals. Start by focusing on either short-term goals, which help you see the smaller details of your academic life, or long-term goals, which help you see the big picture of your academic future. Short-term academic goals are usually helpful when they are focused on your week-to-week academic progress during any given term—for example, setting a goal to complete two chapters of reading for your biology course each week will help you stay on top of your course work. And long-term goals (such as pursuing a major field of study or transferring credits to another institution) can be broken down into smaller goals you want to achieve by the end of each term and year, and by the time you graduate.

---

[4]Doran, T. "There's a S.M.A.R.T. Way to Write Management's Goals and Objectives," *Management Review*, vol. 70, no. 11 (1981): 35–36.

> **QUICK TIP**
>
> **Start with Long-Term Goals**
> It can be helpful to consider your long-term academic picture first because long-term goals can help you define your short-term goals. With the big picture in mind, it's clearer what short-term goals are necessary in order for these long-term goals to be realized.

Step 2: Brainstorm and create your "first draft" goals. To get going, take ten to fifteen minutes to jot down your gut reaction to two questions: What are your long-term academic goals in college? What are your short-term academic goals in college? This type of freewriting can help you begin to identify the main categories that are important to you.

As you respond to these questions, think about the reasons you decided to attend college in the first place. What are you hoping to accomplish academically? Are you interested in a particular field of study, do you want to explore your options, or are you focused on a certain career path? Also consider your values and what's important to you as a person. For example, maybe your health and wellness are a top priority, so one of your goals might be to take a class about nutrition or one that incorporates some sort of physical activity. In addition, consider your own academic strengths and weaknesses so that you can stretch yourself academically, but also set goals that are realistic given your previous academic background.

Step 3: Use the "SMART" method to refine your goals. With your "first draft" goals in front of you, craft SMART goals. A SMART goal has the following characteristics:

1. **It is Specific**, which means it is straightforward and detailed in a way that makes it very clear what you plan to do, why you want to do it, and how it will happen.

2. **It is Measurable**, which means you can define criteria that will indicate your progress as you work toward your goal as well as help you determine when you have achieved your goal.

3. **It is Attainable**, which means that the goal is realistic and something you want to commit to.

4. **It is Relevant**, which means that the goal makes sense in the context of your long-term plans and is something you want to spend your valuable time focused on.

5. **It is Timely**, which means that the present is the right time to focus on the goal and that you can identify a time frame in which the goal can be achieved (as well as checkpoints along the way to assess your progress).

QUICK TIP

Limit the Number of Goals

If you have too many SMART goals, it's easy for them to get lost in the shuffle. As you develop your goals, try to focus on three to five short-term and three to five long-term goals at one time. As you accomplish your goals, figure out if there are other SMART goals you'd like to add to your list.

Step 4: Examine what motivational drivers will help you achieve each SMART goal. SMART goals help you figure out how you want to spend your time and where you want to focus your energy in college. But, movement toward goal achievement only happens if you take action to make it happen. That's where motivation comes in. Reminding yourself of what your academic and personal motivators are will help drive you to accomplish your goal by giving you context for your effort.

Make Your Goals SMART-ER

With your SMART goals laid out, you've created a road map to follow as you tackle your academic life. Remember though, that each day, each week, each month, each term, and each year, things change. College experiences will help you evolve in many ways, and your SMART goals need to evolve with you. So, revisit your SMART goals periodically to make them "SMART-ER" goals.

Evaluate your goals regularly. The "E" in "SMART-ER" indicates the need to evaluate your goals regularly to see if they still make sense and to also evaluate your progress in achieving each goal. For example, your SMART goal may be "Work with a study group in my economics class to focus on problem sets and study for tests each week." While you do end up meeting once a week with other students from your class, you find that you spend more time socializing than actually working and you feel unprepared for the first test. In this case, you may want to redo your goal so it better supports your academic goals.

Redo your goals when necessary. After you evaluate your goal, focus on the "R" in "SMART-ER," which is determining if and how you might want to redo your goal. To stick with the example above, instead of seeking academic support in a study group, you could redo your goal in the following way: "Attend economics weekly review sessions and visit instructor office hours before each test." This process of evaluating and then redoing your goals is a way to check in with yourself about what is and isn't working in your academic life.

✓ "SMARTER" Goals Checklist

- ○ **S**pecific = goals are detailed and specific
- ○ **M**easurable = define criteria to measure progress
- ○ **A**ttainable = goals are realistic and attainable
- ○ **R**elevant = goals are relevant in the larger context
- ○ **T**imely = the timing of each goal makes sense and you have a time frame for its accomplishment
- ○ **E**valuate = evaluate your goals more generally and your achievement progress
- ○ **R**edo = redo your goals if your priorities or motivation changes

CHAPTER 3

Visual Walkthrough

Creating SMART Goals

The chart below details two long-term SMART goals for the academic year and two short-term SMART goals for the term. When crafting your own goals, think about creating a similar chart for yourself to focus your goals and identify your motivational factors.

As you think about your academic goals, remember to incorporate the five aspects of goal creation that make them SMART:

Specific	=	Clarify the what, why, and how.
Measurable	=	How will you measure progress?
Attainable	=	Is it doable and realistic?
Relevant	=	Does it fit with long-term goals/larger academic context?
Timely	=	What is your time frame or deadline?

When crafting your own goals, think about creating a similar chart for yourself to focus your goals and identify your motivational factors.

(1) Break your goals down into long-term and short-term goals.

(2) Write down your "first draft" goal, or what immediately comes to mind. Don't worry about creating a SMART goal right away. You'll be able to refine it later. The purpose here is to capture your gut reaction to what you want to achieve.

(3) Use the "SMART" test to think about how to make your "first draft" goal Specific, Measurable, Attainable, Relevant, and Timely.

(4) Write down what will motivate you to take the steps necessary to accomplish your goal.

① LONG-TERM ACADEMIC GOALS

② First Draft Goal	**SMART Goal ③**	**Motivational Drivers ④**
Earn at least a 3.0 overall GPA	Keep a log of assignment and test grades in each class and work with instructors or go to academic support center if any grade is below a B.	Personal fulfillment from earning high grades; may want to transfer to another college and need a minimum 3.0 GPA to make that happen.
Get to know instructors	For each class, attend office hours for instructors at least two or three times during the term and prepare at least three questions or topics to discuss each time.	Want to feel comfortable getting support from instructors when needed and would like to learn more about research opportunities.

① SHORT-TERM ACADEMIC GOALS

② First Draft Goal	**SMART Goal ③**	**Motivational Drivers ④**
Visit the Writing Center	Schedule an appointment at the Writing Center at least a week before every paper is due to brainstorm ideas, come up with an outline, or get feedback on a draft.	Improve my writing skills by learning from others so that paper writing isn't such a stressful process for me.
Form economics study group	Form an economics study group the first week of classes and then schedule a regular weekly meeting time in library to work on problem sets and study for tests.	Want to learn class material deeply to be able to read domestic and international economics news with an informed eye.

4

Using Time Wisely

Time management is one of the most important, and most difficult, skills to master in college. It may sound simple, but managing time poorly can cause stress and academic problems. If you practice the following three suggestions, you'll be on the right track:

- Keep your daily and academic schedules in one place.
- Write down *everything*.
- Save time by planning and then prioritizing.

Remember: you're in the driver's seat in college. No one is forcing you out of bed in the morning, making you go to class, or checking whether you've started your assignments. And each day is slightly different. For some students, this may be the first time they're in control of their own time; for others, school may be one more responsibility to manage in an already busy schedule. Regardless, it's up to you to make the most of each moment.

LaunchPad Solo
macmillan learning

To access the LearningCurve study tool, video activities, and more, go to *LaunchPad Solo for College Success*. macmillanlearning.com/collegesuccessmedia

55

Time Is of the Essence

Choosing how you spend your time in college is both empowering and a big responsibility. How much should you study? When should you start assignments? How many hours should you devote to reading and to writing papers and labs? And how do you fit all this in without neglecting your other responsibilities—work, family commitments, extracurricular activities, and hopefully some fun?

© Mike Baldwin/CartoonStock.com

Don't fret if you experience some difficulty in managing your time in college. Time management is a skill that you can master. Make it a priority to practice some of the time management tips in this chapter to figure out what works for you.

Given all the activities you have to juggle, you literally have to *spend* time *managing* your time, which will ultimately *save* you time. Within the first term of college, you should try to master certain strategies for effective time management. These time management skills will serve you well throughout your college years and will also be invaluable when you enter the world of work.

Use a Planner

Maybe you have already used a planner, or maybe you didn't need one because your friends had similar schedules or your family members kept you on track. Whatever the case, trying to juggle the many responsibilities of college in your head is a tough job, so using a planner will be invaluable.

Planning will relieve stress. Using a planner leaves less room for error. You are more likely to remember assignment due dates and know when tests are approaching. Staying organized in this way helps you gain control of your daily life and reduce stress as you manage your college responsibilities.

Keeping track. Juggling academics, social life, work, and extracurricular activities isn't easy. But if you plan out each day, you will know how these pieces of your college life fit together. Becoming an expert in organizing your college life takes practice.

With more planning comes more time. It may seem counterintuitive, but the more time you take to plan, the more actual free time you'll have. Keep in mind that while you might view nonclass time as free time, you'll have to spend much of that spare time completing assignments, studying for tests, and fulfilling job and extracurricular responsibilities. In general, for every credit hour you spend in class, you should expect to spend about two to three hours studying (that is, completing assignments and preparing for tests) outside of class. If you take fifteen credit hours per week, you'll probably end up spending thirty to forty-five hours per week studying outside of class, and if you take between seven and eight credit hours, you'll likely spend about fourteen to twenty-four hours per week studying outside of class. Only when you clearly lay out these academic commitments and other responsibilities will your actual free time become apparent.

> **QUICK TIP**
>
> **Relax and Recharge**
> Use your free time to rejuvenate yourself when possible. Take
> time to relax and care for your health, even if it's only for a
> short time. Recharging your battery frequently will make it
> easier for you to successfully juggle your college life and other
> responsibilities.

Choose Your Planner Wisely

You can choose from many types of planners, including Web-based
organizers such as Google Calendar. Some people prefer paper
calendars or bound planners. Other people prefer the planner capabilities on smartphones and iPads. Whatever you choose, it's helpful
to figure out a system that keeps all aspects of your college life in one
place.

Schedule details of your daily life. It's important to write down
everything you need to do each day in your planner:

- Academic life, including class times, labs, instructors' office
  hours, advising meetings, study sessions, and tutoring
  appointments

- Work responsibilities, including shift hours, deadlines for projects, meeting times and any prep work that is necessary, and
  commuting time

- Family commitments, including child care, elder care and
  household responsibilities

- Extracurricular activities, including meetings, hobbies or sports,
  and volunteering

- Personal life, including doctor's appointments, haircuts, social
  gatherings, cultural events, spiritual activities, and exercise

- Relaxation time, including watching your favorite TV show and
  other entertainment, taking a walk or nap, or enjoying quiet time
  by yourself or with friends and family

Make Yourself a Priority

Add mealtimes, exercise plans, and sleep goals to your planner. Doing so can help motivate you to take better care of yourself. For example, if you work much better after a power nap, add a time slot for a nap to your planner so that it becomes a priority.

Add assignment and test details. Most instructors will distribute a syllabus on the first day of class. A syllabus is a road map of the class and contains a variety of important information, including the following:

- The class schedule
- Assignment and required reading due dates
- Test and quiz information
- Instructor office hours

Add this information to your planner for each course so that you have all the essential class details in one place.

Make a plan for studying and completing assignments. Writing down *what day* you will begin assignments and *what day* you will start studying for tests can greatly improve your chances for college success. This aspect of time management—mapping out an assignment and study plan—can mean the difference between quality work and rushed work, or between an all-nighter of cramming for a test and a good night's sleep before taking the exam.

Get started by adding all due dates and test dates to your planner during the first week of classes, and then work backward to determine your start date. As a general rule, start small assignments two to three days before they are due and larger papers and projects at least five to seven days in advance (or more if necessary). Also, begin studying for tests at least three to five days before the test date to be sure you have time to ask questions and understand the material. Since each class is different in terms of assignment and test expectations, check in with yourself as the term progresses to be sure you are giving yourself enough time to complete work and study thoroughly.

✓ Time Management Checklist

1. **Schedule the details of your daily life in your planner:**
   - ○ Academic life (classes, labs, office hours, advising meetings, tutoring)
   - ○ Work life (job hours, staff meetings)
   - ○ Family commitments (child care, elder care, household responsibilities)
   - ○ Extracurricular life (meetings, events, practices, games)
   - ○ Personal life (health care, social engagements, cultural/spiritual commitments, your favorite TV shows)
   - ○ Meals, exercise, and sleep

2. **Add assignment due dates and test dates to your planner:**
   - ○ Readings
   - ○ Papers and speeches
   - ○ Projects
   - ○ Labs and problem sets
   - ○ Quizzes, tests, and exams

3. **Map out your academic plan in your planner:**
   - ○ What day you'll begin each assignment
   - ○ What day you'll start studying for each test

QUICK TIP

Sound the Alarm

Online calendars, such as Google Calendar, can be synched with your phone or other technology devices. That way you'll always have your calendar at your fingertips and can use built-in tools, such as alarm reminders, to help you remember when to go to class, what to prepare for class, when to complete assignments and study for tests, and when you can attend instructors' office hours, along with meeting times, job deadlines, family responsibilities, social events, and so on.

Battling Procrastination

So, your planner is now full of important information—you've detailed your daily schedule, written down important class dates in your planner, and mapped out when you will start these assignments and begin studying for tests. But what if you find yourself procrastinating when you have to start an assignment? A simple but helpful time management tool is a daily prioritized to-do list. Before going into more detail, let's take a minute to consider why you might procrastinate.

Why Do You Procrastinate, and What Can You Do?

Procrastination is a powerful force that most of us deal with daily. It can be especially powerful in college for a number of reasons:

- The academic material you're studying is particularly challenging or confusing, so you would rather put it off or work on easier tasks first.

- You're not interested in the topics you're studying, so it's difficult to motivate yourself to get going.

- Other activities or tasks are more fun than your academic work, so it's easy to put off what you don't want to do.

- You're overwhelmed by the amount of work you have to do, and you don't know where to start.

- Distractions, often in the form of technology, occupy so much of your time that you end up avoiding the work that needs to be done.

This list is not exhaustive, but it might get you thinking about why you procrastinate. In fact, when you find yourself procrastinating, try to acknowledge it. Being honest with yourself about procrastination will actually help you combat it. You can then determine why you're procrastinating so that you can find targeted strategies to overcome your procrastination.

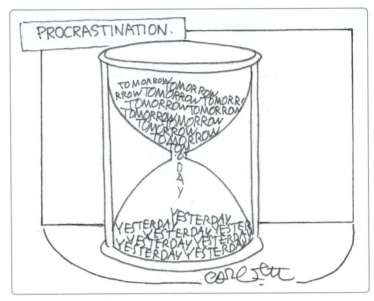

© Jack Corbett/CartoonStock.com

Procrastination can have a cumulative effect if you don't get a handle on it early. Tasks you put off until tomorrow can quickly become tasks you didn't complete yesterday. Instead, take control and use the strategies mentioned in this chapter to manage your workload and not fall behind.

Tackle challenging assignments first. This strategy may seem counterintuitive, but if you work on difficult assignments first, they can feel less threatening and will become easier to accomplish. Moreover, because you're often more focused at the start of study sessions, you'll be at your best.

Build in rewards. In college, as in life, we sometimes have to do things that don't interest us. You can motivate yourself to get started on those types of tasks by rewarding yourself *after* you've completed them.

Include both academic and fun/relaxing activities. All work and no play is not a recipe for success in college. Finding a balance that includes time for academics and time for fun/relaxation will make you happier and more productive.

⑤ **Ways** Smart Students Combat Procrastination

1. Schedule in-person study dates with a classmate to keep each other on task, or connect online using FaceTime or a similar service.

Using your planner to set aside designated study times, especially with other students, will increase your motivation to complete work.

2. Move to a different location if possible when your room or home becomes too much of a distraction, or try out a different study time.

Your room or home may simply feel too comfortable. If you're distracted by the temptation of your bed or noisy roommates, or if it's too difficult to work productively when dealing with family interruptions, try moving somewhere else, such as a library or a coffee shop, or see if trying a different study schedule helps.

3. Set smartphone alarms to remind you to get working.

You probably love using your smartphone, so why not use it to tell you to get going on your work!

4. Give friends and family permission to point out when you're procrastinating.

It can be annoying when others tell you to get working. But if you tell your friends or family that doing so will help motivate you, it just might do the trick, especially if they join you in hitting the books or can help out with child care or household tasks to minimize distractions.

5. Block out a few thirty-minute chunks to enjoy your favorite online sites and respond to e-mail rather than checking them constantly throughout the day.

Dedicating blocks of time for different tasks will increase your productivity and also can give you something to look forward to after you work on assignments.

Break your work into chunks. You can make complex assignments and tests more manageable if you break them into smaller chunks. For instance, divide a ten-page paper into a series of smaller assignments that includes (1) developing a thesis, (2) outlining the paper, (3) writing the introductory paragraph, (4) writing pages one to five, and (5) writing pages six to ten.

Work in intervals and take breaks. Just as you break your work into manageable chunks, break your study sessions into forty-five-minute intervals, each followed by a ten-minute break.

Use a To-Do List

Everyone has a different method for creating a to-do list, but be sure to include everything that you hope to do in a day—including academics, work responsibilities, and personal/family commitments. Academic items on your list might include writing the introduction to a paper, completing a class reading, or studying for a quiz. Nonacademic items might include running an errand, preparing for an organization meeting, working an extra shift, planning your child's birthday party, celebrating your partner's promotion, or even watching your favorite television show.

Prioritize your list. Figuring out what needs to get done first, second, third, and so on can help you avoid procrastination. A list of prioritized tasks serves as a road map. You know exactly where to start, and the list will propel you forward because you have a detailed plan in a particular sequence, without any ambiguity. You also might want to create a symbol system that indicates which items on your list are very important.

Determine what must get done. As you prioritize your list, indicate clearly what must get done that day and what could wait until the following day or later in the week. This step is important because the unexpected will happen and life circumstances may intervene, even if you have the best plan in place. You may not complete every task on your to-do list for a variety of reasons—an assignment may take twice as long as you expect; an emergency may come up at work; you or a family member may get sick; or you may forget about a meeting you needed to attend.

⑤ **Questions** to Help You Prioritize Your To-Do List

1. What assignments and nonacademic obligations are most urgent?

The items that are due the next day, or the deadlines that are one or two days out are most pressing and should be at the top of your to-do list.

2. How can I break down big assignments over the course of a week to ensure they get completed well and on time?

Big projects and papers take time, and it is helpful to make it a priority to complete manageable chunks each day so that you are not overwhelmed with the whole assignment the night before it is due.

3. What exams or quizzes are coming up for me?

Start studying for tests at least three to five days in advance and include this study time on your to-do lists. Remember to make studying a top priority if the test is within one or two days.

4. What tasks could I complete over the weekend or during vacations?

To make your weekly to-do lists more manageable, take off items that are not a top priority and plan to complete them when you have more available time.

5. When do I have longer and shorter amounts of study time during the week?

It's helpful to schedule more difficult assignments or those that usually take you the most time on days you have more study time available, and to schedule items that are easier or take less time during study blocks that are more limited.

CHAPTER 4

Visual Walkthrough

Incorporate To-Do Lists into Your Planner

To get a good sense of what tomorrow will bring, put together your daily to-do list the night before. Then, in your planner, you can note when you'll try to complete each task. For example, after you write your to-do list on Sunday night, look at Monday's schedule and determine when you would like to tackle each item on the list. In creating the to-do list for the next day, be sure to include all new tasks as well as the tasks you didn't get a chance to do the day before.

(1) Note what must get done and what could wait.

(2) Symbols, such as exclamation points and question marks, can flag particularly important items on your list.

(3) Be sure to factor in any commuting time in your schedule as well as identify the flexible time during your day to relax or complete an item on your to-do list.

(4) Indicate where you plan to work on your assignments and study for tests. These location details may affect your schedule if you have to build in travel time.

(5) Your to-do list for the next day will incorporate new items and what didn't get done the previous day.

TO-DO LIST
For Monday   **(1)**
1. Econ. problem set (must finish — due tomorrow) !!!!
2. Study sociology quiz (could wait — quiz Wed.)
3. Write 3–4 pages of 8-page English paper (could wait — due Fri.)
4. Attend econ. office hours (ask about upcoming test) ???
5. Write 1st draft of executive report for boss (get started — deadline Tues.)
6. Check into restaurants for family reunion (could wait — finish by Wed.)
7. Respond to e-mail (important)
8. Exercise (hope to!)

PLANNER	
Monday	
7–8 a.m.	
8–9 a.m.	Breakfast
9–10 a.m.	English class
10–11 a.m.	Sociology class
11–12 p.m.	Economics professor office hours (Hall E, Rm. 301)
12–1 p.m.	Lunch meeting w/academic advisor (Grab N Go Café)
1–2 p.m.	Travel to work and take 20–25 minute walk
2–3 p.m.	Work (10 Main St, downtown) — Write 1st draft of report
3–4 p.m.	Work (10 Main St, downtown)
4–5 p.m.	Work (10 Main St, downtown)
5–6 p.m.	Stop at home & check e-mail/Facebook
6–7 p.m.	Dinner and travel to library
7–8 p.m.	Work on economics problem set (library)
8–9 p.m.	Start studying for sociology if possible (library)
9–10 p.m.	Write Tuesday to-do list & respond to e-mail
10–11 p.m.	TV or Sleep
11–12 p.m.	Sleep
12–6 a.m.	Sleep

TO-DO LIST
For Tuesday
1. Study for sociology quiz (must finish — quiz Wed.) !!!!!
2. Finalize executive report and e-mail to boss (must finish — deadline by end of work day) !!!!!
3. Write 3–4 pages of 8-page English paper (could wait, but try hard to get started — due Fri.)
4. Check into restaurants for family reunion (finish — brothers expecting info. by Wed.)
5. Respond to e-mail (important)
6. Exercise (hope to!)

🔍 case study

Mason describes his struggles with procrastination and how he has helped himself.

The times in college when I struggled with procrastination were when I failed to set clear time frames for when to work and when to socialize or do other activities. The hardest part about college is balancing my own desires and other responsibilities with the need to complete the assignments due the next day. My strategy is to identify where I have the biggest chunk of time, taking into account any classes or meetings I might have during the day. This usually works for me because I tend to work most effectively when I have large periods of time.

My best advice for incoming college students is to start everything early. Homework may not always be fun, but it doesn't have to feel like a chore. If you build homework into your daily schedule, it will feel like the next logical step in the progression of your day.

Something I wish I knew before entering college about time management is the benefit of keeping a physical agenda. I got great advice to do this, but being of this high-tech generation, I decided to keep an online agenda that ended up crashing on me, and I lost everything!

QUESTIONS FOR REFLECTION   When are you most likely to procrastinate? Does the time of day or type of work you're engaged in matter? What distractions are most difficult to ignore? Have you figured out strategies that help you overcome your procrastination tendencies? Are they working? If not, do you need help from an advisor, mentor, instructor, or academic support office?

Finding a Balance

When managing your time in college, you have to make difficult choices in order to find a balance that works for you. You are always faced with competing priorities, and although college is filled with a lot of unstructured time, instructors expect that you will devote most of this unstructured time to academic work. To strike a manageable balance, use your planner as a guide to determine what you can realistically fit in on any given day and in any given week.

Always Start with Academics

As you may have already discovered, the amount of work you are assigned in college is likely greater than what you were assigned in high school. Readings and papers are longer, lab work is more complicated, problem sets are more involved, and tests are more challenging. Because of the volume of work in college, you must schedule time to work on academics every day, spreading out your assignments and studying over the course of the week and the weekend. Your instructors might not assign homework every day, but *you* must assign yourself homework each day, using your planner and the time management strategies outlined in this chapter.

Your Schedule Will Lead the Way

By using a planner that allows you to see how much academic work you need to do each day and each week and also factoring in your work and family obligations, you'll have a better sense of what else you can add to your life. You might even realize that you need to cut back on extracurricular activities or job hours, if that's possible. Organizing your time in a planner will help you make these important decisions.

In college, you need to make many decisions: How many hours can you realistically devote to your job? Should you consider becoming a leader in an on-campus organization, given the additional hours required for the position? When will you fit in exercise? Do you have time to add an extra class to your schedule, and if so, do you have enough hours left to complete assignments and study for tests? Your planner, which outlines your daily and weekly schedule, will be invaluable as you assess what you can and cannot handle.

All Work and No Play Isn't a Good Solution

Students do their best work when activities that bring joy and fulfillment are also part of their daily routine. When you're assessing your daily and weekly schedule, try to carve out some time for fun, relaxation, physical activity, or a meaningful hobby or passion. This can be difficult when work and family demands are pressing, but even a little fun or relaxation can go a long way to relieving some stress. Look at your planner to determine how much time you have for enjoyable activities, and then find an activity that matches both your interests and how much time you can devote to it. For example, if you enjoy dance but have only two hours a week available, try to find a one-hour dance class that's offered twice a week, or if you love cooking for family or friends, schedule a weekend evening for a special dinner.

Be Flexible

Your circumstances may change at any time during the term, so it's important to stay flexible when developing your schedule. Remember: the details in your planner are not set in stone. For example, you might need to change the amount of time you devote to a particular class if you find that the course work is more challenging or time consuming than you expected. Similarly, you may need to adjust your schedule if you're struggling in a class and realize that you need regular tutoring sessions. If you need to increase your job hours, you might need to cut back on the number of hours you devote to extracurricular activities.

Whatever the case, as you master the skill of time management, you'll be better able to find a balance that works for you—a balance that keeps you not only busy and productive but happy as well.

QUICK TIP

Revisit Your To-Do List Periodically

If you need to, be ready to rework your to-do list and assignment schedule by moving whatever didn't get done to another day so that you don't forget to complete these tasks, and be realistic about commute times and transition times so you're not always rushing or late. Being flexible and realistic will also help you manage any unforeseen circumstances that may arise.

part

II

Study Skills

5

iStock.com/CagriOgner

Learning Preferences and Studying

Y ou may have noticed that you learn better depending on the way in which material is presented or the way in which you study. Maybe engaging in hands-on activities helps you understand new information without a problem. Or maybe you get more out of studying with others than you do studying alone. There are various assessments available to help you better understand yourself, aid your academic decision making, and inform your study methods, including the two we will examine in this chapter: VARK and the Myers-Briggs Type Indicator.

The process of figuring out your personal learning and study preferences can be very powerful because it helps you make better academic choices and develop strategies that will allow you to stay more engaged in class and study more effectively. This understanding can help you see multiple perspectives so that you can adapt to academic situations that may be initially uncomfortable for you, and will also allow you to feel more personally invested and fulfilled throughout college.

LaunchPad Solo
macmillan learning

To access the LearningCurve study tool, video activities, and more, go to *LaunchPad Solo for College Success.* macmillanlearning.com/collegesuccessmedia

73

What Is VARK?

The VARK questionnaire helps people understand their learning preferences based on these four sensory modalities: Visual, Aural, Read/Write, and Kinesthetic. Specifically, the questionnaire sheds light on how people prefer to digest information and communicate their learning. Before you can understand your learning profile, you need to determine your VARK preferences. The test is available online; just type "VARK Questionnaire" into a search engine to access the questionnaire.

Understanding the VARK

Once you have taken the VARK test, you receive a score that tabulates how many questions you answered that correspond to each sensory modality. For example, your score might look like this:

Visual: 4

Aural: 3

Read/Write: 8

Kinesthetic: 1

In this case, read/write is your preferred learning preference given the number of questions you answered that tie to the read/write modality. If, however, your scorecard indicates two modalities with similar scores (for example, visual: 6; aural: 7; read/write: 2; kinesthetic: 1), you are multimodal and prefer two sensory modalities almost equally. Let's define each modality so that you can understand how to use your VARK score in the classroom and while studying.

Visual (V). The visual modality is a preference for visual representations, including images such as charts, graphs, diagrams, photographs, maps, symbols such as arrows and circles, and other visual illustrations that show patterns or shapes. Those with a visual preference are not necessarily drawn to words that are written on a board with just a shape around them. Instead, they prefer symbols used to *connect* the words in some meaningful way.

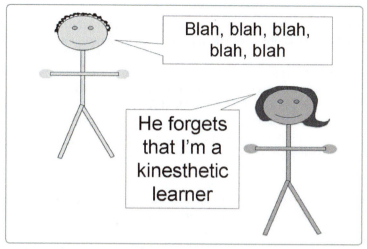

© 2009 Linda M. Farley

Some of your college courses may not fit your learning preferences; when this happens, try to be flexible. Think creatively about how you can incorporate your learning preferences in a way that is appropriate and helpful, possibly by engaging with the material in a meaningful way after class.

Aural (A). The aural modality focuses on listening, or what can be heard or spoken. Those with an aural (auditory) preference find it easier to digest and understand information by listening. They learn well through lectures, speaking out loud, group and class discussions, and Web conferences.

Read/Write (R). The read/write modality is all about words. People with this preference learn better through the written word—whether it's the act of writing or the act of reading.

Kinesthetic (K). The kinesthetic modality is a preference for hands-on, real-world learning with a physical component, such as personal experiences, vivid examples, or simulated or real practice. Kinesthetic learners want to *do* something to learn a concept, such as an experiment, or prefer to see a live demonstration in order to experience the learning in a concrete way. Students with a kinesthetic preference learn better when they engage one or more of their senses.

I Know My VARK Score: Now What?

Once you receive your VARK score and understand which sensory modalities you prefer, you need to learn how to put your preferences to work for you in college. It's important to remember that they are not set in stone and that none are "good" or "bad"; in addition, your preferences are on a continuum and can be influenced by situations and circumstances. While you will find you will need to learn to adapt your learning preferences to fit many different situations in college, it's important to find ways to engage your personal preferences in order to use strategies tailored for you.

Choose classes that align with your preferences. When picking classes, be sure to consider your VARK learning preferences. For example, if you are an aural learner, try to choose discussion-based courses; the audible back-and-forth of class conversation will aid your learning. If you have a visual preference, try to find an instructor who relies heavily on visual representations to relay information during lectures. If you have a reading/writing preference, look for an instructor who gives mostly reading- and writing-based assignments. And if you are a kinesthetic learner, you might do particularly well in courses that provide opportunities for hands-on work, such as science classes with labs.

Learn to adapt. You will have to take a number of college courses that don't align with your learning preferences, so it's important to find ways to adapt. One good strategy is to take class notes in a way that draws on your preferences. For example, if you have a visual preference, use visual representations in your notes; if you are an aural learner, read your notes out loud after class. When you are learning course material, try to make use of your VARK preferences. For example, if you are a kinesthetic learner, try to engage several of your five senses in the material by developing your own experiment or personalizing the material. If you have a reading/writing prefer-ence, look for additional readings on the course's subject matter. And if you are multimodal, try a few different ways of taking notes in class in order to find the one that works best for that particular class. Talk to your instructor if you find yourself struggling to adapt. Together, you might think of a creative way to tackle an assignment or strategies to stay more engaged during class.

QUICK TIP

Expand Your Horizons

College is a time to expand your horizons, so don't be afraid to take classes that don't fit your learning preferences, especially if you are interested in the subject matter. Stepping out of your comfort zone allows for growth and will help you develop skills and strategies to succeed in situations that might be uncomfortable. You will experience many uncomfortable situations in college and after college, so being willing to take a risk and learning how to adapt are important life skills.

Use preference-specific study techniques. Studying in college is complicated because there are so many ways to study and so many different types of classes to study for. To increase your understanding of material and to improve your test scores, determine what study techniques might complement your VARK preferences. You may study most effectively by using flash cards, rewriting your notes, acting out scenarios, drawing visuals, or discussing material with your instructor or peers. Play to your strengths: choose the study techniques that work best for you and most aligns with your learning preferences. See the Visual Walkthrough in this chapter for specific strategies on how to incorporate your VARK preferences in your study sessions.

✓ **Checklist for How to Use Your VARK Learning Preferences to Your Benefit**

○ Try to find classes that fit your learning preferences.

○ Take notes in ways that draw on your learning preferences.

○ Use study techniques that complement your learning preferences.

○ When classes don't fit your learning preferences, find ways of incorporating your learning preferences into assignments or study techniques.

CHAPTER 5

Visual Walkthrough

Use Your VARK Learning Preference during Study Sessions

While studying for tests, draw on your VARK learning preferences to increase your understanding and retention of material. To better retain the information in this example reading, follow the suggestions for your particular learning preferences and apply these tips to your other course readings.

process for food, clothing, building materials, and many other purposes. Most likely, these first Americans wandered into the Western Hemisphere more or less accidentally, hungry and in pursuit of their prey.

African and Asian Origins

Human beings lived elsewhere in the world for hundreds of thousands of years before they reached the Western Hemisphere. They lacked a way to travel to the Western Hemisphere because millions of years before humans existed anywhere on the globe, North and South America became detached from the gigantic common landmass scientists now call **Pangaea**. About 240 million years ago, powerful forces deep within the earth fractured Pangaea and slowly pushed continents apart to approximately their present positions (Map 1.1). This process of **continental drift** encircled the land of the Western Hemisphere with large oceans that isolated it from the other continents long before early human beings (*Homo erectus*) first appeared in Africa about two million years ago. (Hereafter in this chapter, the abbreviation *BP* — archaeologists' notation for "years before the present" — is used to indicate dates earlier than two thousand years ago. Dates more recent than two thousand years ago are indicated with the common and familiar notation *AD* — for example, AD 1492.)

More than 1.5 million years after *Homo erectus* appeared, or about 400,000 BP, modern humans (*Homo sapiens*) evolved in Africa. All human beings throughout

MAP 1.1
Continental Drift
Massive geological forces separated North and South America from other continents eons before human beings evolved in Africa 1.5 million years ago.

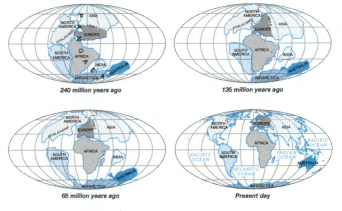

240 million years ago   135 million years ago

65 million years ago   Present day

- **Visual learners.** Keep a pen and paper handy to draw visual representations, symbols, and diagrams of the information you're learning. Draw a timeline re-creating important information in the maps, and include relevant details from the text.

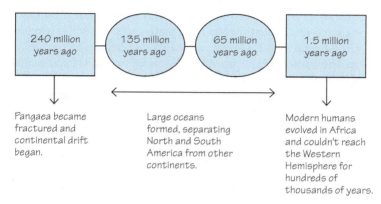

240 million years ago

135 million years ago

65 million years ago

1.5 million years ago

Pangaea became fractured and continental drift began.

Large oceans formed, separating North and South America from other continents.

Modern humans evolved in Africa and couldn't reach the Western Hemisphere for hundreds of thousands of years.

- **Aural learners.** Ask your instructor whether you can record lectures and then play them back while you are studying. Read the important details of the text out loud, discuss the material with an instructor during office hours, and ask study group members to quiz you on the material.

- **Read/Write learners.** Write notes in the margins that highlight important points. Also, write your understanding of the material in your own words:

   "Modern humans evolved 1.5 million years ago in Africa, and because continents drifted apart long before humans existed (240 million years ago), humans didn't set foot in the Western Hemisphere for hundreds of thousands of years. Humans didn't have a way to travel across the oceans that separated North and South America from the rest of the continents (these oceans formed between 65 and 135 million years ago)."

- **Kinesthetic learners.** To engage several senses, ask an instructor for a movie that illustrates the concepts detailed in the reading. Think of real-world examples that tie directly to the concepts you are learning. Or demonstrate the continental drift shown in Map 1.1 in a concrete way: create different continents out of clay, and move them at million-year intervals in a pan of water, representing the oceans separating North and South America from the other continents.

What Is Myers-Briggs?

The Myers-Briggs Type Indicator (MBTI) is another tool that can help you understand your learning preferences. The MBTI identifies the different aspects of your personality that define who you are and how you interact with others. Knowing your MBTI personality type can clarify the ways in which you prefer to learn and can help you make informed choices in college that can lead to improved academic performance.

Similar to the VARK questionnaire, the MBTI test reveals your personal preferences based on your responses to a series of questions. The MBTI has four scales, each of which has two classifications:

1. Extraversion (E) or Introversion (I)
2. Sensing (S) or Intuition (N)
3. Thinking (T) or Feeling (F)
4. Judging (J) or Perceiving (P)

The MBTI test results will indicate that you have a moderate or strong preference for one of the two classifications within each scale. Sixteen different combinations or personality types are possible:

ISTJ	ISTP	ESTP	ESTJ
ISFJ	ISFP	ESFP	ESFJ
INFJ	INFP	ENFP	ENFJ
INTJ	INTP	ENTP	ENTJ

The MBTI test will indicate where you rank in each classification. For example, you might have a very strong tendency toward extraversion and demonstrate little tendency toward introversion, but you might fall somewhere in the middle on the thinking/feeling scale, with thinking tendencies just slightly outweighing feeling tendencies.

Taking the MBTI test is the best way to determine your personality type, but you can get a general sense of your MBTI personality type by reading the brief descriptions of each classification in the next section.

QUICK TIP

Take the MBTI

Some colleges offer opportunities to take the MBTI test, often through the Career Services Office (or an equivalent office). If your college does not offer the MBTI test, go to the Myers & Briggs Foundation Web site to find other ways to access the test. Professionals must be certified to administer, score, and interpret the MBTI test properly, and several Web sites provide this service, usually for a fee.

Personality Type Can Influence College Choices

Once you understand the definition of each Myers-Briggs classification, you can determine how to use this information to assist your learning throughout college. Knowing your Myers-Briggs preferences can help you make informed academic decisions.

Extraversion versus Introversion. This scale indicates how people prefer to interact with the outside world. An extravert gains energy not only from being around people but also from being actively engaged with them. At the other end of the spectrum, introversion is a tendency to look inward. An introvert gains energy from thinking about ideas inside his or her head and values and seeks time alone.

- **Extraverts** enjoy classes that allow for active class participation and group discussions because they are comfortable speaking in groups and are stimulated in these situations. They prefer instructors who facilitate lively and active discussions and debates. In addition, they seek opportunities to work on group projects because their learning is enhanced in the presence of others.

- **Introverts** tend to be drawn to classes that allow for deep introspection and individual work. They prefer instructors who lecture without too much class discussion, opportunities to speak one-on-one with instructors, and assignments that focus on individual thought rather than group collaboration.

Sensing versus Intuition. Sensing types and intuitive types differ greatly in how they interpret, digest, and analyze information. Those with a sensing preference are detail-oriented pragmatists who use the five senses and focus on facts. Those with a preference for intuition, by contrast, look beyond physical reality to the meaning that can be interpreted. They believe that "gut feelings" and "intuition" matter more than what can be gathered from the five senses.

- **Sensing** types are often interested in courses that are fact based and have practical applications, such as science, math, and economics. They prefer learning opportunities and assignments that draw on all five senses, such as experiments, labs, and experiential learning.

- **Intuitive** types are drawn to classes that offer open-ended discussions and to assignments that allow them to unravel the meaning behind concepts and ideas. They like to focus on big-picture topics.

Thinking versus Feeling. People with these two classifications differ in the way they make decisions and in what factors they consider important in making decisions. Thinking types analyze the pros and cons of a situation and try to weigh both sides fairly, without letting emotion get in the way. Thinkers value logic and rational analysis of facts. Feeling types, however, tend to make decisions with the heart, rather than with the head. They try to understand how their decisions will affect other people because they want to do what's best for those involved.

- **Thinking** types prefer classes that require analytical skills. Thinkers want to apply general principles and rules whenever possible. They seek out instructors who value and reward this type of thinking and who give assignments that ask students to look at both sides of an issue using logic rather than emotion.

- **Feeling** types often excel in classes that provide opportunities to understand and think about how people are affected by situations and events. They particularly enjoy subjects such as psychology, sociology, and history. Feelers like to make judgments with their hearts, so they are drawn to instructors who value analysis that brings in personal emotions and reactions.

Judging versus Perceiving. This scale indicates how people prefer to structure their life. Those with a judging tendency have a preference for making decisions. Judging types find comfort when things are settled and planned rather than left uncertain. By contrast, perceiving types like to stay flexible and spontaneous, taking in information readily and easily.

- **Judging** types prefer well-organized classes and assignments with clear guidelines and predictable deadlines. They appreciate instructors who present information in a clear and concise way and who stick to an outline.

- **Perceiving** types are usually drawn to classes that allow for freedom and creativity. They seek out instructors who are flexible and who don't mind deviating from the syllabus. Perceiving types prefer classes without clear right or wrong answers so that they can explore all angles of a problem without boundaries.

© Dan Reynolds/CartoonStock.com

Knowing your MBTI type is a powerful tool as you make decisions throughout college. Judging types tend to be quick decision makers and follow through on plans, while perceiving types take a wait-and-see approach and reflect on the information they receive. Which one are you?

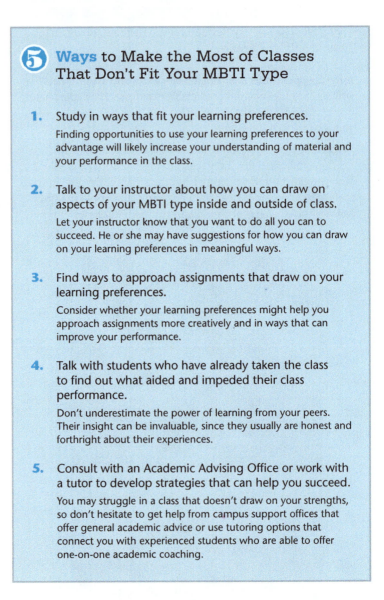

5 Ways to Make the Most of Classes That Don't Fit Your MBTI Type

1. **Study in ways that fit your learning preferences.**

Finding opportunities to use your learning preferences to your advantage will likely increase your understanding of material and your performance in the class.

2. **Talk to your instructor about how you can draw on aspects of your MBTI type inside and outside of class.**

Let your instructor know that you want to do all you can to succeed. He or she may have suggestions for how you can draw on your learning preferences in meaningful ways.

3. **Find ways to approach assignments that draw on your learning preferences.**

Consider whether your learning preferences might help you approach assignments more creatively and in ways that can improve your performance.

4. **Talk with students who have already taken the class to find out what aided and impeded their class performance.**

Don't underestimate the power of learning from your peers. Their insight can be invaluable, since they usually are honest and forthright about their experiences.

5. **Consult with an Academic Advising Office or work with a tutor to develop strategies that can help you succeed.**

You may struggle in a class that doesn't draw on your strengths, so don't hesitate to get help from campus support offices that offer general academic advice or use tutoring options that connect you with experienced students who are able to offer one-on-one academic coaching.

🔍 case study

Audrey explains how her learning preferences affect her college experience and how she studies.

I learn most effectively and have the most rewarding experiences in classes that fit my learning preferences in one way or another. I prefer an intimate classroom setting where I can actively interact with the instructor and other students via discussions, team collaboration, and group projects, instead of sitting through a long lecture in which information has to be absorbed passively without an active exchange of ideas. But I've gotten a lot out of large lectures by taking notes in a more visual way that keeps my brain more engaged and improves my understanding of the material.

For classes and subjects that don't fit my learning preferences, I have figured out that incorporating my learning preferences while studying is key to my understanding and helps me perform better on assignments and tests. I like to form small study groups to engage in one-on-one conversations about class material and to be able to test each other out loud. I also draw as many visual representations in my study notes as possible to help me retain information.

QUESTIONS FOR REFLECTION   Are you taking classes that don't fit your learning preferences? If so, how are you performing in these classes? Can you think of ways to draw on your learning preferences during class or while studying to improve your performance? What strategies can you employ to make the most of classes that don't fit your learning preferences? Be sure to try out these strategies and determine which are the most successful for you.

Study with Your Learning Preferences in Mind

Studying in ways that are in tune with your learning preferences is a powerful way to aid your college learning. Whether or not you studied a lot, a little, or not at all in high school, you'll need to develop different study habits in college to do well. Why? One reason is that although you have to memorize some material, studying solely by memorizing information won't be effective in college. College tests require a deeper understanding of the material—an understanding that asks you to apply theories or facts to novel problems and questions, or to make connections and draw conclusions that may not be obvious. For example, it's not enough to memorize the definition of a principle in economics. Instructors expect you to have a deeper understanding of the principle and will ask you to apply the principle to problems you've never seen or talked about before. Another thing to consider is that exams are usually less frequent in college than in high school, so the amount of material covered in each exam is much greater. Therefore, knowing how to study in college and how to incorporate your learning preferences while studying are essential skills. Fortunately, it is one that you can master through planning, making connections, and using various study tools.

Create a Study Plan

If you take five or ten minutes to develop a study plan, studying for each test will feel less overwhelming. Here are some tips to follow to get started.

Start with time management. Once you receive a class syllabus, use your planner to establish your study schedule for all exams and tests. Plan to begin studying at least three to five days before a test to be sure that you have enough time to cover all the material and to ask questions if you don't understand something. Giving yourself some extra time means that you'll be prepared in case the unexpected happens, such as getting sick, and you won't have to stay up all night cramming the day before a test.

I REALLY CRAMMED LAST NIGHT.

© Ralph Hagen/CartoonStock.com

Although cramming for tests the night before may seem like a good study strategy, it doesn't give your brain enough time to fully retain the material. Try studying over the course of a few days to make sure that you completely understand the information and have time to ask questions, instead of overloading your brain with last-minute studying.

Determine time and location. If you study at a time when you focus best, you're likely to do more than memorize. And location matters, too. Try to find a spot that minimizes distractions and maximizes your concentration, and take your learning preferences into consideration. For example, perceiving types enjoy studying in an environment that is constantly changing (such as a student center) and that allows creativity to flow, while judging types prefer a more structured, predictable environment. Once you've determined your ideal study time and location, add this information to your daily to-do list.

Make a list of what you need to study. This can include lecture notes, readings, problem sets, and assignments. For judging types, a clearly laid out to-do list will come naturally, but this may not be as intuitive for perceiving types who prefer less structure. So if you're not sure what to put on your study list, talk to your instructor or classmates to narrow it down.

Use study tools. As you consider the study tools available to you, figure out how to incorporate your learning preferences. In other words, there are ways to keep your learning preferences front and center when writing study notes, studying with others, and taking practice tests that will improve your understanding and retention of material.

Prioritize your list. This will help you determine where to start and how to keep yourself moving through the material. How you prioritize your list depends on your preferences. For example, you might decide that you'd like to study all your lecture notes and then all your readings. Or you might mix it up a bit for variety. It can be helpful to study lecture notes and readings that are connected or on the same topic so that you can determine how the information from various sources is related.

QUICK TIP

Study Difficult Material First

If you are struggling with certain concepts, theories, or readings, study those first. Why? Your brain is usually at its best when you first begin studying, and it may take you more time to fully understand this type of material. Another important advantage of starting early is that if you still have trouble understanding the material, you'll have time to get extra help before the test.

Make Connections with Study Notes

To develop a deeper understanding that allows you to successfully tackle test problems you've never seen before or to discuss information in novel ways on exams, take study notes that highlight important connections. Study notes are additional notes you take while you are engaging in the process of studying for tests, and they will engage your brain more fully because you're not just rereading or skimming; instead, you are meaningfully writing while thinking deeply about the material. Your study notes will facilitate critical thinking if you keep the following ideas in mind.

Create meaningful chunks. Can you group information into meaningful categories or sort it into contrasting categories? Categorizing in a certain way for a specific reason will be particularly useful for MBTI thinking types, who learn best when they can test their understanding by applying rules or logic to material. And for all other types of learners, this process of grouping is equally important—because the more you pull information into coherent chunks, the more connections your brain is making, thus making it easier for you to recall the information on tests.

Incorporate your learning preferences into your notes. The more you can examine the material using your personal learning preferences, the more likely you are to understand and remember it. For example, if you are a visual learner, creating diagrams, charts, graphs, or pictures of information in your study notes that visually connect details will help you view the material in a new way, improving your retention. Or if you are a read/write learner, the simple practice of writing and rereading your study notes will enhance your grasp of the material. Similarly, if you are a sensing type, you will benefit from processing this information through multiple senses, such as speaking your notes out loud or redoing a hands-on experiment and writing down your results in your study notes. Alternatively, if you are an intuitive type, personalize the material by bringing in your personal reactions and experiences.

Study with Others

Forming a study group can help you and your classmates grasp important concepts. Be thoughtful about how many students you want to include in the group. Sometimes studying with just one or two other people is enough to test your understanding of the material. If you are an introvert you may be more comfortable studying in a small group, and if you are an extravert you might prefer having multiple voices at the table to help you engage in a meaningful dialogue with more opportunities for interaction.

Come prepared. Make the most of your study sessions by figuring out beforehand what you want to cover during the study group meeting. Your study group might choose to focus on a particular topic, concept, theory, or reading, or on material you are having difficulty understanding. This is particularly important for introverts who will likely get more out of the study session if they have had time to think deeply about the material on their own beforehand. And for judging types, being prepared and organized will allow for greater focus and engagement, since the time together will be used efficiently.

Ask questions and debate. Asking and answering questions will reveal how well the students in your group know the material you're studying. If you have trouble responding to a question, you'll know which material you need to revisit before the test. Engaging in a debate is also useful because it forces you to think thoroughly about the material, especially if you're trying to form arguments and responses on the spot. You should expect that college tests will require you to think on your feet, and practicing this type of thinking in a study group will improve your performance. This strategy may work particularly well for extraverts, but introverts can also participate comfortably if they prepare beforehand by thinking about the material and bringing points to discuss to the study group session. Feeling types will benefit by incorporating examples that involve people in meaningful ways to aid their understanding and retention.

Practice individually, then discuss. Always come prepared to group study sessions by bringing practice problems and questions to answer and discuss. Given the different learning preferences that are likely in the group, first work on the problems and questions individually; then talk about your answers as a group. This technique can highlight what each member does and doesn't know, can help introverts feel more willing to participate, can aid sensing types who benefit from engaging multiple senses, and also can reveal different perspectives or approaches to the problems and questions.

Collaborate virtually if that is helpful. A virtual study group that "meets" through a technology platform can be just as effective as one that involves talking in person. Keep this possibility in mind, especially if you and your classmates don't live near one another. It is important to make the time to engage with others on the material you're studying.

Take Practice Tests

Taking practice tests will help your performance on actual tests. The results of a practice test will reveal which topics or concepts you don't know well enough. You'll also find out if you're struggling to recall information fast enough to complete the test in the time allotted.

To create your own practice tests, talk to the instructor about the test format, such as the number of questions and types of questions, and reference old assignments and quizzes you've taken in the class. Identify the key topics and most important information you'll need to know for the exam, then compile and create questions that focus on these areas. For example, if you are creating a practice test for your engineering class, test yourself on practice problems, or, for your history exam, come up with essay questions that ask you to incorporate and synthesize relevant historical details.

Once you've taken a practice test, go back and check your answers, paying close attention to what you got wrong, what you struggled to answer, and what you couldn't answer. Grading your practice test will provide a road map for the topics and concepts you need to study more thoroughly before the actual test. Then, use study tools tailored to your learning preferences to study the material you don't know. And then, if you still don't understand some of it, get some help from classmates or your instructor.

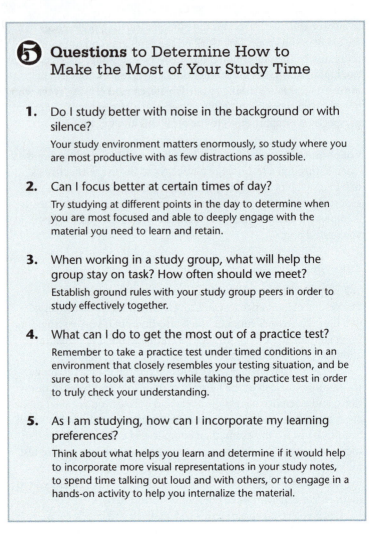

5 Questions to Determine How to Make the Most of Your Study Time

1. Do I study better with noise in the background or with silence?

Your study environment matters enormously, so study where you are most productive with as few distractions as possible.

2. Can I focus better at certain times of day?

Try studying at different points in the day to determine when you are most focused and able to deeply engage with the material you need to learn and retain.

3. When working in a study group, what will help the group stay on task? How often should we meet?

Establish ground rules with your study group peers in order to study effectively together.

4. What can I do to get the most out of a practice test?

Remember to take a practice test under timed conditions in an environment that closely resembles your testing situation, and be sure not to look at answers while taking the practice test in order to truly check your understanding.

5. As I am studying, how can I incorporate my learning preferences?

Think about what helps you learn and determine if it would help to incorporate more visual representations in your study notes, to spend time talking out loud and with others, or to engage in a hands-on activity to help you internalize the material.

6

iStock.com/CagriOgner

Critical Thinking

I t's likely that at some point in your life a teacher has asked you to "think critically" or to use "critical thinking skills." But what does the term *critical thinking* really mean? According to Dictionary.com, *critical thinking* is defined as "the mental process of actively and skillfully conceptualizing, applying, analyzing, synthesizing, and evaluating information to reach an answer or conclusion." This is a thorough definition, but it might sound a bit overwhelming. Don't worry, however. Critical thinking can come naturally if you practice *how* to be a critical thinker. In this chapter, we'll explore how to become a critical thinker and apply those skills to all aspects of your personal and academic life, such as considering new information in your courses, problem solving, decision making, and even creativity. Becoming a critical thinker will not only help you become a better learner, but also will continue to be an important skill long after you leave college and begin your career.

LaunchPad Solo
macmillan learning

To access the LearningCurve study tool, video activities, and more, go to *LaunchPad Solo for College Success.* macmillanlearning.com/collegesuccessmedia

93

Critical Thinking in College

All aspects of college academic life—attending lectures, visiting instructors during office hours, completing assignments, working in study groups—require that you use critical thinking skills. College instructors expect that you will think more critically and carefully than you ever have before. Simply regurgitating what you read in textbooks or what you hear during lectures is not enough. Instructors want students to think freely and analytically, to ask questions and offer a fresh perspective, and to be willing to think outside the box. What instructors want is critical thinking.

In fact, critical thinking is at the core of a college education. Colleges are in the business of educating for many reasons. One important reason is to help students become active and engaged citizens of our society. To be truly active and engaged in a job, within a local or global community, in a school system, in politics, or in any other arena, people must think deeply about whatever information and experiences they encounter. Colleges want students to develop critical thinking skills so that they can evaluate information and their experiences by exercising careful judgment, offering novel insights and ideas, challenging the status quo, and asking insightful questions—essential life skills.

Five Steps for Critical Thinking

To become a critical thinker in college, you need to develop certain traits that characterize this type of deep thinking. The following five steps will help you make critical thinking a natural reflex. You might want to refer back to this list periodically, whenever you encounter a new academic situation.

Step 1: Ask a lot of questions (and answer them!). Asking questions is a key aspect of critical thinking. Asking and answering questions will help you clarify details, clear up confusion, and push for a deeper understanding of the material. When you ask questions, the material will become more meaningful because the questions you ask will matter to you. Asking questions will also help you remember the information. Why? Asking thoughtful questions means that you're a thinking and engaged participant rather than a passive observer.

For example, as you're reading material or listening to a lecture, continually ask if you understand what is being argued or presented. If not, ask yourself what is causing your confusion, and get answers. In a class debate, ask your classmates what evidence they have for the arguments they're making. During an instructor's office hours, explain why you think the assigned readings complement or contradict one another; then ask whether your instructor agrees or disagrees with your assessment.

Step 2: Evaluate your own reactions. Do you agree or disagree with the information being presented? Why? This type of evaluation pushes your thinking to a deep and personal level. By critically evaluating your reaction to the material, you're asking yourself not only whether an argument makes sense but also whether you believe it. Whether you agree or disagree, it's important to ask yourself why.

For example, do you think your instructor's lecture was compelling? If you agree with the instructor's arguments, ask yourself what evidence convinced you and why. If you disagree, ask yourself what evidence was suspect and why. If you don't fully understand or agree with your instructor's arguments, what additional questions should you ask? What do you need to do to dig deeper into the topic and come to a conclusion? Meeting with your instructor during office hours to discuss your reactions to the course material is also a great opportunity to exercise your critical thinking.

Step 3: Analyze the information with a "critical" lens. During lectures or when you read, try to poke holes in the argument and ask whether anything is missing. Has any evidence or information been forgotten, covered up, or ignored? College is an ideal time and place to be thoughtfully skeptical about what you're hearing and reading. Obviously, you won't be able to poke holes in a number of things—laws of physics, mathematical theorems, well-proven theories. However, no academic discipline is a perfect science. College is the time to push back and be thoughtful about the information you encounter.

For example, after you analyze aspects of the information presented during a lecture, do you think important material was left out, oversimplified, or minimized? Would different examples or other

"Are you sure this photo is of us? It looks like a couple of floating logs to me."

Critical thinking in college requires analysis that digs deeper into material than what may be on the surface. Practice being a skeptic and taking a deeper look at everything you read and hear.

kinds of evidence have altered your understanding of the instructor's argument or perspective? If you're skeptical of aspects of a lecture, why do you think that's the case? Do readings offer a diverse or complementary perspective that clarifies your thinking?

Step 4: Make connections and keep the big picture in mind. You're bombarded with a lot of information in college. To be an effective critical thinker, take the time to step back periodically and synthesize what you're learning in order to see the big picture. Synthesizing (which means combining different aspects of the information in a coherent and meaningful way) while also making connections between different types of material can clarify what is most important.

For example, connect your instructor's lectures with what you're reading in the class. Instructors assign readings for a reason. By thinking critically about why the readings are important and how they relate to the instructor's lectures, you're expanding your understanding of the material in important ways. You might realize that a reading's argument differs from the instructor's position on the subject. Which side makes more sense to you and why? The key is to apply what you're learning in the class's various components—lectures, readings, and assignments—to the bigger picture of the course as a whole.

Step 5: Apply your learning to your own life experiences. All of us are shaped by our past learning and experiences. The more you can bring your past experiences into the college learning process, the more powerful your critical thinking skills will be. If you personalize material and make it matter to you, you're more likely to think deeply.

For example, consider how your past shapes the way you look at information, the reasons you agree with certain aspects of an argument, or why you have specific types of questions. Did a past class significantly influence your thinking on the topic? If so, why? Have you had particular experiences—travel, activities, internships, jobs—that have shaped your perspectives? Asking *why* the material is important to you is an interesting question to answer.

> **QUICK TIP**
>
> **Bring "You" into the Equation**
> If you're taking a required class that you didn't choose, try to figure out how the material is relevant to your life. By bringing "you" into the equation, you will care more, think more deeply, and perform more successfully.

The five steps in this process are in no particular order. You may (and should) ask questions while you think critically about information. Or you may simultaneously evaluate your reaction to material and consider how the past informs your thinking. You don't have to do the steps in any strict sequence; rather, this five-step process is intended as a guide you can use to further develop your skills as a critical thinker.

> ### ✓ Critical Thinking Checklist
>
> ○ **Conceptualize** material fully by asking questions frequently and finding answers.
>
> ○ **Evaluate** your reaction to material by asking whether you agree or disagree with it and why.
>
> ○ **Analyze** material by being critical of all perspectives and by asking what is missing.
>
> ○ **Synthesize** material to make connections and examine the big picture.
>
> ○ **Apply** what you're learning to past experiences in order to better understand your reactions to material.

Try Not to Inhibit Critical Thinking

Engaging in critical thinking isn't easy. Students sometimes hold beliefs that inhibit or limit their critical thinking. For example, it's natural to assume that your instructor or a textbook author knows everything and that you don't know anything. As a result, you might tend to be a passive observer during lectures and while you read, taking everything as fact. But agreeing with everything prevents you from thinking critically about the information presented. It's fine to agree, but ask yourself *why* you agree and whether you have found enough evidence to support your decision to agree.

🔍 case study

Maryann shares her perspective on developing critical thinking skills in college.

Once I arrived at college, I realized that my courses required more in-depth analysis and interpretations than I was used to and that I had to adjust my critical thinking skills. I discovered that the ways I used to read and write were going to have to change drastically. As an avid reader and highlighter fanatic, I quickly realized that writing my "philosophical" college essays required more than just taking extensive marginal notes. I had to really think, immerse myself in the material, and redraft my conclusions as my analysis of the evidence changed.

My critical thinking skills continue to develop each day, adjusting to different aspects of my social and academic life. And I've realized that critical thinkers are in search of "a truth," while also understanding that there are many ways in which to interpret things. Also, when you are using critical thinking skills, whether you're writing an essay or participating in discussions in class, there is no specific road map to follow because everyone comes at the material from different perspectives. And it does help to become passionate about something because the way in which you use your thinking skills will be grounded in your personal beliefs, making the material matter more.

QUESTIONS FOR REFLECTION   Is the level of critical thinking required in your college courses different from what was expected of you in high school or at your previous or current job? Do you understand how to be more critical in your thinking? If you're not sure, get help by talking with an advisor, your instructors, or a staff member in an academic support office on campus.

Another common pitfall is ignoring your reaction to the material presented because you assume that it doesn't matter if you agree or not. However, your perspective is not only valuable but also new. Sharing and understanding your reactions to material will enhance your thinking and might even influence other students, creating a more meaningful learning experience.

Moreover, try to ask any questions you have, even if you're afraid of looking foolish. It's easy to feel intimidated in college, especially as a first-year student, but if you're not asking questions, you're not engaging in critical thinking. At the very least, ask questions one-on-one during your instructor's office hours or with peers you trust.

"You're the best teacher I've ever had. You opened my eyes to the world and showed me how to think critically... I was *happy* until I met *you*."

Remember to stay in tune with your instructor's expectations as you engage in critical thinking. Be a critical thinker who offers a novel perspective, constantly analyzes material, and asks insightful questions, but also understand what you need to do to succeed in the class. If you need some help with critical thinking, talk to your instructor.

⑤ Questions to Help You Build Your Critical Thinking Muscles

1. What is my immediate reaction to this?

Write down your immediate reactions to lectures, class discussions, and readings without censoring your thoughts.

2. What is the other side of this argument?

When a topic is being debated or discussed, come up with counterarguments even if you agree with what is being said. Stretch yourself to consider more than one side of the debate.

3. What questions do I have about this material?

Before each new class session, write down three questions you might want to ask about the material that already has been covered.

4. How does this material connect to what I've already learned?

At the end of each class, find two ways the material could be connected to previous classes and write that in your notes.

5. How does this relate to my life?

During study sessions, figure out if there is at least one way the material could meaningfully relate to your life, and share that with a classmate.

QUICK TIP

Think for Yourself

When you work with a study group, be sure to think as an individual. It's easy to assume that the groupthink that arises out of your study group discussion is the only way to think about an issue. However, don't let the group limit your own critical thinking, especially if you feel unsettled by conclusions that the study group makes.

Where to Use Your Critical Thinking Skills

The five steps for critical thinking, although general, can be applied to all of your academic experiences in college. Try using the five steps, in any order, while reading class assignments, completing problem sets, researching and writing papers, participating in group projects, and listening to lectures. Instructors will expect you to think critically in each of these academic endeavors, so take note of the specific ways critical thinking can be applied to reading, writing, informational literacy, and note taking in the chapters that follow.

In addition to academics, you can apply your critical thinking skills to everyday college life—whenever you are solving problems or making decisions—and throughout any creative process.

Critical Thinking while Problem Solving

Good problem solving depends on critical thinking, so keep in mind a few rules of thumb when you're trying to solve a problem. First, understand the root of the problem; next, gather and analyze any information to help you solve the problem; and finally, brainstorm several possible solutions to the problem before determining which solutions are best.

Understand the root of the problem. Take the time to determine where the problem is coming from. What exactly are you trying to solve? For example, if you're having an academic problem in a class and want to figure out what to do, consider the possible roots of the problem. Are you struggling to understand the professor's lectures, get through all the assigned readings, or finish timed tests? By uncovering the roots of the problem, you'll be more likely to find the right solution.

Gather and analyze information. Determine what information or resources would help you and then take time to step back and reflect. For example, let's say that your academic problem is difficulty completing tests in the time allotted. Let's say, further, that during

⑤ **Ways** You Use Critical Thinking in Everyday College Life

1. When making choices about how to spend your time outside of class.

College life can be complicated, especially if you have a job, a family to care for, or both. Because you are likely juggling quite a few tasks and responsibilities, you need to be very thoughtful about how you spend your time.

2. During a class discussion.

Whenever you're involved in a class discussion in which different sides of an argument are being evaluated, you're using critical thinking skills.

3. While working on a new fundraiser for your favorite student organization.

To have a successful fundraiser, you need to be creative and to analyze what has and hasn't worked in the past—all evidence of critical thinking.

4. When deciding whether to switch majors.

Before switching majors, you will need to weigh the pros and cons of the decision. You have to ask and answer many important questions to be sure you think deeply about what you really want to do.

5. While discussing your future with an advisor or mentor.

Conversations about your future can be intense and require deep introspection. Honestly examining your past and present experiences, as well as keeping your mind open to possibilities, will push your thinking in new ways.

your information gathering, you find that most other students are not struggling to finish the same tests. And you recognize that in the past you have had trouble with timed tests, particularly in the same subject. You also often get stuck on a few problems and then go blank, making it difficult to complete the remainder of the test. Gathering and then analyzing this information helps you recognize that the tests aren't unusually long (because others are completing them in time); rather, you realize that you're struggling to understand aspects of the material and are experiencing test anxiety.

Brainstorm possible solutions. To continue with our example, if you think carefully about your analysis of the problem, you can find many possible solutions, including meeting with the instructor to get additional help with the material and to discuss test-taking strategies. Another solution might be to spend more time studying. You might decide it would be worthwhile to form a study group, visit an academic support office, or investigate the possibility of working with a tutor.

With possible solutions in mind, use your judgment to determine which one would work best. If more than one solution could be effective, you can use trial and error to determine the best one. However you choose to solve the problem, keep these strategies—understanding the root of the problem, gathering and analyzing information, and brainstorming a variety of possible solutions—in mind to help you engage in critical thinking throughout the problem-solving process.

Critical Thinking When Making Decisions

Critical thinking is a fundamental part of decision making as well as problem solving, and the rules are similar—clarify the decision you're making; gather and analyze any information that will help you make the decision; and brainstorm and weigh the pros and cons of each possible alternative before making a decision.

Clarify the decision. Simplify the decision-making process by stripping away aspects of the decision that are irrelevant. For example, if you're trying to pick a major, think about the fields you are *not* interested in. Then you'll be left with the majors that are relevant—making your decision easier and clearer.

Gather and analyze information. Let's say you conclude that you're most interested in majoring in psychology, sociology, or English. Then, determine what information will help you differentiate among these three majors. For example, how many classes in each major sound particularly interesting? What makes the classes interesting? If class size matters to you, check how many students will be taking the various classes because some majors tend to have larger classes than others. Talk to fellow students majoring in each field, as well as instructors, to get a better feel for the majors. And consider how your career aspirations might influence your decision.

Weigh the pros and cons. Keeping in mind the information you have gathered, list and then weigh the pros and cons of each possible option. To continue with our example, if you conclude that the average class size in the psychology department is larger than you prefer but that you're most interested in the psychology classes and have learned about exciting research opportunities you'd like to pursue, majoring in psychology might be the right decision. If you also realize that you are nearly as interested in English as in psychology, you might decide to pursue English as a minor.

Whatever the case, remember to engage your critical thinking skills throughout the decision-making process. When you engage in this type of thorough thinking, you'll be more satisfied with your decision.

QUICK TIP

Take Time to Reflect

Take time to reflect after you've chosen a solution to your problem or made a decision. Continue to be a critical thinker by evaluating how things are going. Is your solution working? If so, why is it working? If not, should you consider other solutions to the problem? After making a decision, are you happy with it? If not, can you change your decision to make things better?

CHAPTER 6

Visual Walkthrough

Be a Thoughtful Decision Maker

There will be many decisions you'll have to make in college—academic, social, personal—that require a good deal of deliberate thought. Push yourself to be a thoughtful decision maker by using the critical thinking steps below.

1. Reframe the decision in a way that helps you fully understand what the decision is really about.

2. Detail the basic (and sometimes obvious) information you must consider when making an informed decision. Analyze what's possible after examining the information you have laid out to further your critical thinking.

3. Be very honest about the pros and cons to ensure you are examining and weighing all angles of the decision.

4. After making your final decision, sleep on it if you can and then revisit your decision making process the next morning to see if it makes sense and feels right.

Decision 1: Should I accept an unpaid research internship in a psychology lab?

Decision 2: Should I reduce the number of classes I take next term to part-time?

1 **CLARIFY THE DECISION**

I need to decide if I want to perform extracurricular research by working with psychologists in the department I am majoring in.

Given my mom's health, it would be helpful for me to be at home in the early evenings. Since I work 20 hours a week and am taking a full credit load at school, I need to decide if I should reduce my class schedule.

- The internship hours are M/W/Th 2 to 5 p.m.
- The lab is a 15-minute commute.
- Internship is related to my academic focus — mind/brain/behavior
- I have a paid job at the gym T/W/Th from 6 to 9 p.m.
- I currently volunteer as a mentor in a local school on M/F from 2 to 4 p.m., which presents a conflict.

- I need to help at home between 4 and 8 p.m. on M/W/F.
- I work from 4 to 8 p.m. each day, but there is another work shift available from 7 a.m. to 12 p.m. I could switch to.
- I could take one class after lunch on M/W/F and one class in the evenings on T/Th (when my aunt is able to help out at home).

③ **WEIGH THE PROS AND CONS**

Pros:
- The research opportunity would give me experience in a lab setting.
- Instructors would get to know me and could write strong recommendations.
- My commute time is not an issue.
- I could still work at the gym.

Cons:
- Internship is unpaid and I would be adding another 8 to 10 hours of "work" to my schedule.
- I would have to give up my volunteer position because two days a week are required to stay in the mentoring program.

Pros:
- Moving to a part-time class schedule would allow me to move my work schedule from the evenings to the mornings.
- Reducing my class load would give me more flexibility in my schedule.

Cons:
- Becoming a part-time student will delay my path to graduation and getting a full-time job.
- Two classes I won't be able to take as a result of moving to part-time may not be offered next semester.

④ **FINAL DECISION**

Although this position is unpaid, it's convenient and would help me as I figure out my future career path. To make Wednesdays and Thursdays more manageable, I will see if I can switch my work hours at the gym to Fridays and Sundays.

I will reduce my class load this term to help out at home. But I will take a few classes each summer, which will help me stay more on track for graduation. And I will check into home care options for my mom to see if additional help could be brought in during the week to care for her.

Critical Thinking and Creativity

You might wonder why the concept of creativity is relevant in a chapter about critical thinking. In fact, creativity and critical thinking are intricately linked. You need to be creative when engaging in aspects of critical thinking, such as coming up with examples that clarify an idea, trying to poke holes in a well-supported argument, and developing new or alternative explanations. And critical thinking is essential when you are being creative because as you come up with novel ideas or explanations during the creative process, you need to analyze whether the ideas and explanations make sense, can be well supported, and are relevant.

In college, you can be creative in many ways—while writing a paper, working on a group project, organizing a club event, engaging in research, debating a topic, or discussing a lecture with an instructor. Think critically throughout any creative process by taking the time to question, analyze, and evaluate what you are creating. And when you engage in critical thinking, don't lose sight of the power of creativity in improving and expanding your thought process.

7

iStock.com/CagriOgner

Note Taking

I t's the second week of class, and you're sitting in Economics
101 with your laptop for extensive note taking. The instructor
begins to lecture, and you start taking notes. But how do you
listen and take notes at the same time? Is it better to write down
everything word-for-word and then later figure out what the
instructor said? What if you can't get everything down? Are
notes all that useful anyway?

Even though note taking isn't easy or the most exciting topic, it
is important. Notes help you make sense of what you're learning by
pulling together concepts and revealing your instructor's perspective
on the subject. In that way, notes are an invaluable academic tool
you can constantly refer back to. Taking good, well-organized notes
does take effort, but it will save you time when you go to study or
complete an assignment. In college, developing the habit of taking
useful notes, which involves a great deal of critical thinking, is a
useful skill that will enhance your learning and understanding of
course material.

LaunchPad Solo
macmillan learning

To access the LearningCurve study tool, video activities, and more, go to *LaunchPad
Solo for College Success*. macmillanlearning.com/collegesuccessmedia

109

Take Thoughtful Notes

Many students assume that critical thinking is relevant to readings and assignments, but not to other academic situations. For example, you might view lectures as a time to sit back and just listen, taking notes on whatever the instructor says but not thinking critically about the lecture. When you sit passively, though, it's easy to lose focus, making it difficult to recognize whether you truly understand what's being said. Once the class is over, you move on to your next activity and don't give a second thought to the material presented in the lecture.

In college, the information presented during class is integral to your learning and to your academic success, so it's important to be thoughtfully engaged during class. College instructors expect that students will think carefully and deeply about the material and perspectives that are presented as well as about any noteworthy research that is discussed. Note taking is a way to stay actively engaged, but taking thoughtful notes is possible only if you can fully concentrate throughout class.

Set the Scene

To help yourself concentrate and stay engaged, try to set yourself up for success. Be sure to complete assigned readings before each lecture so that you are familiar with what will be covered. Being prepared will help you stay more focused because you will have already mulled over topics and issues that might be discussed.

Another way to prepare for a lecture is to ask yourself big-picture questions: Where does today's topic fit into the wider themes of the class? Is this lecture a continuation of something that was discussed previously, or will the information be new? Do I already know something about the material being presented?

Determine what distractions hinder your learning in class so that you can eliminate them. If you tend to fall asleep in class, figure out what will help you stay awake. If you get restless in class and sometimes feel as though you want to get up and walk around, think of ways you can subtly release your energy without distracting other students.

© Andrew Toos/CartoonStock.com

Part of good note taking is making sure that you are fully engaged in the lecture. It's easy to let distractions get in the way of your learning in college, but it's up to you to figure out how to help yourself stay focused.

It's not always possible to stay focused when you need to. Maybe you're dealing with a family problem, or you've heard some exciting news and can't wait to celebrate. If something distracting causes you to lose your focus in class, be proactive: ask a classmate if you can borrow his or her class notes, or visit your instructor during office hours. If you find that being distracted is a chronic problem, something more serious might be going on. Don't hesitate to get help from an advisor, mentor, or someone in the Academic Advising Office or similar resource at your school.

QUICK TIP

Clear Your Head

Unexpectedly, you can be confronted with difficult life situations, making it tough to concentrate. When this happens, take a few minutes before class to write down what's on your mind and what actions you might take to deal with the issue.

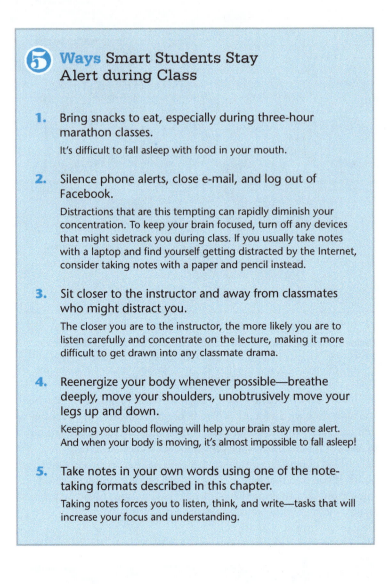

⑤ **Ways** Smart Students Stay Alert during Class

1. Bring snacks to eat, especially during three-hour marathon classes.

It's difficult to fall asleep with food in your mouth.

2. Silence phone alerts, close e-mail, and log out of Facebook.

Distractions that are this tempting can rapidly diminish your concentration. To keep your brain focused, turn off any devices that might sidetrack you during class. If you usually take notes with a laptop and find yourself getting distracted by the Internet, consider taking notes with a paper and pencil instead.

3. Sit closer to the instructor and away from classmates who might distract you.

The closer you are to the instructor, the more likely you are to listen carefully and concentrate on the lecture, making it more difficult to get drawn into any classmate drama.

4. Reenergize your body whenever possible—breathe deeply, move your shoulders, unobtrusively move your legs up and down.

Keeping your blood flowing will help your brain stay more alert. And when your body is moving, it's almost impossible to fall asleep!

5. Take notes in your own words using one of the note-taking formats described in this chapter.

Taking notes forces you to listen, think, and write—tasks that will increase your focus and understanding.

View Lectures as Conversations

A useful technique for taking thoughtful notes in class is to pretend that each lecture is a conversation between you and the instructor. If you view the lecture as an exchange of ideas and thoughts, you become an *active* and *important* participant, rather than a passive observer. Your notes, then, are a place to write down your "lecture conversation." But what exactly should you write down?

Capture the main ideas. Write down the main ideas and important takeaways that are presented in class, including any opinions, perspectives, or research the instructor discusses.

Write down examples, evidence, and anecdotes, as well as formulas, equations, and sample problems. These details will shed more light on the material being discussed for better understanding and will serve as important reference material to return to throughout the course.

Highlight anything the instructor repeats. Whenever your instructor emphasizes certain points by repeating or summarizing them, be sure to write them down in your notes—this is information your instructor wants you to remember.

React to the information. Do you agree or disagree with what the instructor is saying? Why? What is your opinion on the material? Does the information presented make sense to you? Is anything missing? Throughout the lecture, write down your analysis or evaluation of the material your instructor is presenting.

Determine what questions you have. In your notes, write down any questions you have about the material presented in the lecture. After class, get answers to these questions from your instructor, or discuss the questions with your study group.

Writing down your personal reactions, analysis, and questions in your notes will keep you more engaged because you are responding to the lecture conversation that is unfolding throughout the class. To make any conversation meaningful, you need to listen actively and then ponder, react, and ask questions along the way. Unlike a conversation you might have with a friend, though, this exchange of ideas and questions happens in your notes.

> **QUICK TIP**
>
> **Use Your Own Words**
> You don't need to write down every word the instructor utters. In fact, if you merely transcribe a lecture, you are only passively engaging in the class. You're so busy writing down every word that you're not thinking critically about what's being said. Instead, try to take notes using your own words.

Note-Taking Styles

There is no "right way" to take notes—you can choose from many note-taking formats. If you're a linear thinker or a list person, you might prefer to take notes straight down a page. If you're a visual learner, you might want to add charts or visual representations to your notes as the instructor speaks. Whatever note-taking style you use, remember to write down your reactions, analysis, and questions. If you add this layer of personal reflection and evaluation to your notes, you will listen more critically to the lecture and will take more thoughtful notes.

Instructor Notes

Your instructor might provide a handout (usually in the form of an outline) as an overview of the class or as a framework for your note taking. Use this document to guide the way you take notes in class. Either on the handout or in a separate document, take additional notes in your own words. These notes will add more detail to whatever the instructor has already included on the handout. And, as with any notes you generate on your own, be sure to write down your personal reaction, analysis, and questions as well.

Your Personal Style of Note Taking

It's important to take notes that work for you, so feel free to add your personal touch. You can combine the formats described in this chapter, depending on the information being presented and your learning style. For example, to aid your understanding, you might add visual notes to your outline, or combine a table of notes with diagrams.

PENCIL AND PAPER?! TALK ABOUT *OLD SCHOOL!*

Notes are useful only if they are in a style and format that work for you. Don't worry about what your neighbor is doing, unless you think it will help you understand and engage with the material more fully.

You might use different note-taking styles in different classes. For example, you might prefer to make graphical representations of theories in your economics class, but in your psychology lectures, to take notes in an outline format. Whatever the case, the more you personalize your notes and make them your own, the more likely they are to aid your understanding and studying, thus improving your academic performance.

Taking notes critically and thoughtfully requires effort, but the payoff is huge. Because this type of note taking takes concentration and engagement with the material, you'll have a more thorough grasp of the course. In addition, you'll find it easier to complete assignments and study for tests. When you stay focused during class, you won't have to relearn everything from scratch.

Visual Walkthrough

Using the Table Format

The table format is easy to use if you are taking notes by hand or on a computer. Simply create a table with three columns: the first column for class notes, the second column for your reaction to the class material, and the third column for questions you have during class.

(1) The first column is for notes that focus on the substance of what the instructor is saying. Use this column to write shorthand notes in your own words that highlight the important points the instructor is presenting, including concepts, theories, facts, principles, arguments and supporting evidence, examples, and anecdotes.

(2) The second column is for your personal reaction, analysis, and opinions about the class material. This section is important because it adds a layer of critical thinking to your notes. You might want to consider such matters as, whether you agree or disagree with what's being said, whether any information appears to be missing, and how your life experiences influence and inform your response to the lecture.

(3) The third column is for any questions you have during or after class. For example, if you don't understand a theory the instructor presents, highlight it in your notes so that you remember to discuss it with the instructor during office hours.

VIETNAM WAR: ON THE HOME FRONT

① Class notes	Reaction/ Analysis ②	Questions ③
Mass movements against the war * Students for a Democratic Society (SDS) — Recruited 20,000 people; first major demonstration in DC; SDS chapters at more than 300 college campuses; protests against ROTC, CIA, military research projects, manufacturers of war material * Martin Luther King Jr. — Rebuked US government as "the greatest purveyor of violence in the world today" * Environmentalists — Disgusted by use of chemical weapons (e.g., Agent Orange)	Mass movements were necessary to get president's attention (unfortunate it had to get to this level).	Where did the SDS movement start, and how long did it take to spread to so many campuses?
Antiwar sentiment * Media questioned war — New York Times (1965), Wall Street Journal & Life magazine (by 1968), Walter Cronkite * Prominent Democratic senators urged negotiation instead of force — J. William Fulbright, George McGovern, Mike Mansfield * Women Strike for Peace (WSP) — Founded 1961; worked for nuclear disarmament; alerted public to horror & danger of the war	Important that media took a stand, given media influence in US — must have made a real impact — find out more.	Want to know more about Senate's role in de-escalation of the war — Republicans vs. Democrats?

Visual Walkthrough,
continued

Using the Outline and Cornell Formats

The outline and Cornell note-taking formats help you organize details presented during class, including important concepts, theories, facts, principles, arguments and supporting evidence, examples, and anecdotes. This format is helpful for material that is highly structured, but it can be used for any class or note-taking situation. Include your personal reactions, analysis, and questions in your notes—preferably in the margins to keep your outline clear and concise. Finally, summarize your notes at the bottom of the page and take time to reflect and read over your notes on a weekly basis. This will make it easier to review key information when you study.

(1) This example provides a rough sketch of how you might use elements of the outline and Cornell note-taking formats to organize information presented during a history class focused on the Vietnam War.

(2) The main topic—"On the Home Front"—is broken down into major topics (I. and II.).

(3) Subtopics (a, b, c, etc.) help clarify the information in the main topic.

(4) Relevant details (i, ii, iii, etc.) expand on the subtopics.

(5) In the margins, add any reactions, analysis, or questions you might have.

(6) Also after class, summarize your notes at the bottom of the page.

VIETNAM WAR: ON THE HOME FRONT

Mass movements were necessary to get president's attention (unfortunate it had to get to this level).

Where did the SDS movement start, and how long did it take to spread to so many campuses?

I. Mass movements against the war
   a. Students for a Democratic Society (SDS)
      i. Recruited 20,000 people
      ii. First major demonstration in DC
      iii. SDS chapters at more than 300 college campuses
      iv. Protests against ROTC, CIA, military research projects, manufacturers of war material
   b. Martin Luther King Jr.
      i. Rebuked US government as "the greatest purveyor of violence in the world today"
   c. Environmentalists
      i. Disgusted by use of chemical weapons (e.g., Agent Orange)

Important that media took a stand, given media influence in US — must have made a real impact — find out more.

Want to know more about Senate's role in de-escalation of the war — Republicans vs. Democrats?

II. Antiwar sentiment
   a. Media questioned war
      i. *New York Times* in 1965
      ii. *Wall Street Journal* by 1968
      iii. *Life* magazine by 1968
      iv. Walter Cronkite
   b. Prominent Democratic senators urged negotiation instead of force
      i. J. William Fulbright
      ii. George McGovern
      iii. Mike Mansfield
   c. Women Strike for Peace (WSP)
      i. Founded 1961
      ii. Worked for nuclear disarmament
      iii. Alerted public to horror and danger of the war

Summary:
On the home front, antiwar sentiment and mass movements against the Vietnam War escalated, which served to alert the public to the realities of the war and get the president's attention.

Visual Walkthrough, continued

Adding Visuals

You can make your notes more visual in a number of ways: Draw simple diagrams with circles and arrows that connect material. Create flowcharts to visualize information, especially if the material has a natural sequence or flow. Or use an information map, in which key concepts appear in the center of the map and notes radiate from those key points. The following examples transform aspects of the outlined notes into visual formats.

DIAGRAM

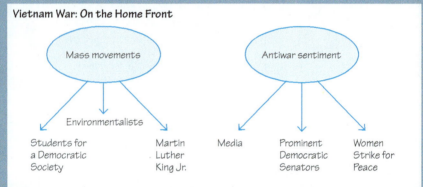

FLOWCHART

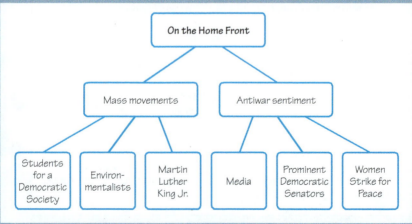

Q case study

Lucas shares his note-taking preferences.

In high school, I didn't take notes very often and still did well on tests, so when I started my first year of college, I thought notes weren't important. When it came time to study though, I realized that I had forgotten a lot of key details from the lectures. So my instructor suggested I learn about note-taking strategies before the next text.

I figured out that the most effective way I take notes is to use an outline format with headings followed by bullet points. Most of the time, this system works well, but it definitely depends on the class. For example, in classes such as biology, I had to learn more visually, so drawing diagrams really helped my learning. I also recognized that taking notes is especially important when I'm trying to put the "puzzle" of the class together. Because I can constantly refer back to my notes, I'm better able to see how the class topics connect and to tie readings to material the instructor has explained.

QUESTIONS FOR REFLECTION   If you're using the same note-taking style for each of your classes, would trying a different note-taking style in any of them help you understand the subject matter better? Do you ever read over your notes after class? If you have a question about your notes, what do you do?

Review Your Notes Early and Often

Most college students leave a class and don't think about it again until it's time to study for a test, complete an assignment, or visit an instructor during office hours. But you can improve your critical thinking and retention of class material by taking ten minutes later in the day to read over your notes. This strategy is an effective way to synthesize what was said during the lecture and to begin to imprint the material on your brain. Remembering to *also* read over notes from previous class sessions while reviewing your new notes is especially helpful when it comes to retention, and this will increase the connections you make between material discussed on different days.

Answering these critical thinking questions, whether at the bottom of your daily notes or in a separate section of your notes, will not only deepen your understanding, but is a great way to figure out what you don't understand or what you'd like to investigate in greater detail. Some of your questions might be answered by using class readings, reviewing previous class notes, or doing outside research. But other questions might require a meeting or online exchange with your instructor, a teaching assistant, or a classmate. Either way, it's better to get answers to your questions early on, rather than having unanswered questions the night before an exam.

A final note-taking suggestion: take a few minutes *before class starts* to read over your notes from the last lecture. This strategy will help you remember where the discussion left off and will help you make connections between different class topics and readings. It will also focus your mind on the current class, rather than the class you had earlier in the day. This strategy provides a few more moments of critical thinking as you assess the big picture of the course, giving you more time to make connections and highlight important details in your mind.

QUICK TIP

Make Connections

Connect your notes to assigned readings. Notes provide a bridge between what you're learning in class and what you're reading outside of class. If you don't understand why your instructor assigned a particular reading, consult your lecture notes. Thoughtful notes should help you determine how the lectures relate to the readings and vice versa.

⑤ Questions to Answer after Reviewing Your Notes

1. What are the key takeaways from class and why are they important?

If you don't know, review your notes until you can easily detail the important parts of class.

2. Do I agree or disagree with the information presented? Why?

This question provides an opportunity for reflection, and as you push your thinking deeper through reflection, it will become easier for you to make contributions to class discussions.

3. Is anything missing from the evidence, or unclear from the examples provided?

Answering this question will broaden your understanding of the material as you think outside the box and determine if there is other information to consider and explore.

4. In what ways does the information connect to previous class discussions?

Thinking about this will help you see the big picture of the course and will make studying for tests easier, since you will have already gained practice in connecting material throughout the course.

5. How does the material relate to me and my past experiences?

Personalizing the material makes it matter more and leads to easier retention and a more meaningful class experience.

Checklist for Effective Note Taking

- Find a location in class that helps keep you engaged.
- Practice techniques that increase your focus—turn off devices that may be distracting, breathe deeply, eat a snack.
- Take notes on the instructor's arguments and supporting evidence, examples, theories, facts, and anecdotes.
- Take notes on your personal reactions, analysis, and questions along the way.
- Read over your notes after class and add anything salient.
- Ask yourself "critical thinking" questions about class.
- Get answers to anything you don't understand or want to investigate further.

8

iStock.com/CagriOgner

Reading Effectively

M aybe you enjoy reading and do it for fun or maybe reading is the last thing you want to do. Whatever you study in college, instructors will ask you to read textbooks and other supplementary materials so it is in your best interest to learn strategies to read more effectively. The amount of reading assigned in college can be extensive and may come as a surprise. And college reading is often denser than the reading you did in high school. It's normal if you find your reading assignments overwhelming. Sometimes the sheer number of pages you need to get through is the challenge; at other times, the complexity of what you are reading poses difficulty. Whatever the case, you can take certain steps to help you manage it all, understand your reading assignments, and succeed in your courses. By tackling reading assignments in a less daunting way and by actively engaging with the reading through asking questions and taking notes, you'll be well on your way to mastering the material.

LaunchPad Solo
macmillan learning

To access the LearningCurve study tool, video activities, and more, go to *LaunchPad Solo for College Success*. macmillanlearning.com/collegesuccessmedia

Set Yourself Up for Success

With any assignment in college, your mindset matters because it will influence the level of concentration and focus you're able to give. With college-level reading in particular, you need a certain level of engagement with the material; otherwise, the reading exercise is a waste of time. It's easy to read words on a page, but if you finish and realize you have no idea what you've been reading, you're not in the right frame of mind.

Location Matters

You can help yourself by finding a location that improves your focus. If you always fall asleep while reading in bed, it's best to find another place to read. Through trial and error, you might determine that a special spot in the student center, with the constant hustle and bustle as background noise, keeps you focused. Or maybe dead silence in the library is what you need.

Break Down Readings

Extensive college reading assignments can feel overwhelming. A simple yet effective strategy to make readings more manageable is to break them down into chunks over the course of one day or even a few days. It's much easier to envision yourself finishing twenty-five pages of reading rather than plowing through a hundred pages. And if you read smaller segments, you'll find it easier to check your understanding of the reading.

QUICK TIP

Take Steps to Help Yourself
If you stop after doing some reading and find that you haven't retained much, it won't help to continue. Figure out why you might be having trouble and take steps to help yourself. If you're distracted, find another location or read later in the day. If the text is too challenging for you, meet with classmates or an instructor to get some help.

"This is a 'text book', it's a bit like a website but printed on paper."

© Gary Cook/CartoonStock.com

We're so used to constantly using our electronic devices that college textbooks might feel a bit foreign. Just remember to break down long readings into smaller chunks to make them more manageable.

Remember Time Management

If possible, read when you're most alert. Use your planner to detail when and where you plan to complete your reading assignments each day. Also use a daily to-do list to help you divide your readings into manageable chunks. For example, you might split your reading into three twenty-five-page segments that you plan to finish at three different points over the course of two days. Recognize when it takes you longer than expected to get through a reading, and adjust the amount of time you'll need to set aside for similar types of reading assignments in the future.

Read Effectively

Once you're ready to dive into your college readings, it's not enough to read the words and move along. Reading effectively means retaining the material. This will help when you need to recall details during class discussions and when you study for tests. The type and length of college reading will vary by subject and class, but you can apply effective reading strategies to any assignment.

Before starting a reading, look through the text, noting aspects that catch your eye, such as highlighted text, images, diagrams, section titles, and summary sections. Scanning the text makes you more familiar with the material before you start reading, and can aid your understanding since your brain will begin processing aspects of the information presented. Moreover, these text markers often point to essential information that you'll need to remember.

Engage with Your Reading

Engage with your readings as a critical thinker. You will read more effectively if you apply the five steps for critical thinking as outlined below.

Step 1: Ask questions frequently. Before you begin to read, ask where the reading fits into the course as a whole (to provide context for the material). While reading the text, check your understanding by periodically pausing and asking yourself questions: Is this an important detail? Can I fully picture the example provided? What evidence supports the argument? Do I remember the theory I just read?

Step 2: React as you read. Evaluate the text as you read, checking whether it makes sense, and gauge your opinion of the arguments presented, the examples given, and the effectiveness of the author's writing. If you're reading a scientific piece, examine the experimental procedure and statistics to be sure they are sound.

Step 3: Ask what's missing. Critically analyze the information presented to decide if anything might be missing. This step will also help you think about whether the information is biased in a particular direction. For example, if other viewpoints and examples had been included, would you view the text differently?

Step 4: Think about the big picture. As you read, make connections between different parts of the text and other readings. Are there ways to synthesize the arguments of multiple readings to highlight salient aspects of class? Then, take it a step further by making connections to class lectures and assignments.

Step 5: Personalize the text. While reading, consider how your personal experiences inform your understanding of the material. As you're reading, what matters to you and why? How do your experiences help you understand and interpret the reading in a unique way?

These steps are intended to guide your thinking while you read. Some of the steps might be more relevant than others, depending on the reading assignment. But with practice, this type of critical thinking will become a natural part of your reading process.

✓ Effective Reading Checklist

○ Ask questions frequently while you read.
○ Evaluate the text while you read.
○ Ask yourself what's missing from the text.
○ Connect the reading to the big picture.
○ Personalize the text whenever possible.

Take Notes

To fully engage yourself while reading, take critical thinking notes along the way. Write down your questions and reactions, take note if you think a perspective is missing, outline your synthesis of the text clearly, and don't forget to personalize the text. You might decide to

⑤ **Ways** to Clarify Confusing Reading Material

1. Look back at class notes to see if the instructor has discussed readings or topics related to readings.

Instructors assign readings for a reason and often touch on aspects of readings during class, so your notes may shed light on material that is confusing.

2. Step back and consider the other readings that you have been assigned, and make comparisons and/or connections to the confusing material.

By reflecting on how multiple readings may speak to each other—either through similarities or differences—you can attain a new understanding.

3. Ask yourself if class assignments or experiments could provide insight into the confusing reading.

Thinking through an assignment or reflecting on the process and results of experiments may provide a lens to help clarify what is confusing you.

4. Meet with peers, teaching assistants, or instructors.

Sometimes a conversation with another person who is able to explain or even demonstrate the material in a different or unique way makes all the difference.

5. Consider using academic resources, such as a visit to your Academic Advising Office or a similar source of support at your school.

If you still struggle after trying a number of ways to clarify the material, there may be more going on that academic resources could help you identify, such as an undiscovered learning disability. It might mean finding a tutor you meet with regularly if that's an option at your school.

take notes in the margins of the reading, on a separate piece of paper, or on a computer.

Use symbols. Using symbols while you take notes on a reading can help your reading process. For example, you might use an exclamation point to represent your agreement, draw a circle around examples, add a question mark if you don't understand something or if you find some evidence questionable, and use arrows to indicate aspects of the text that connect in some way.

Take time to slow down and really understand what you're reading. The more thorough and deliberate you are while reading and taking notes, the more powerful your understanding and retention of material will be.

Visual Walkthrough

Take Critical Thinking Notes while You Read

Taking notes that push you to think critically while you read will help you better understand and retain the ideas and information in the text. Moreover, you'll be able to refer back to your reading notes when you study for tests or if you need to use the text for assignments or projects. Reading different types of textbooks will require you to use different types of strategies, too. For example, while reading a humanities textbook, you'll have to sift through a lot of text in order identify key concepts and central ideas, while a science textbook might require you to apply concepts through exercises. In either case, you'll want to approach your textbook reading with intention. We will explore both a humanities and science textbook example in this Visual Walkthrough.

Reading a Humanities Textbook

(1) Underline main ideas and key concepts.

(2) Take summarizing notes in the margins.

(3) Circle specific examples.

(4) Use question marks when you have a question or don't understand something in the text.

(5) Use exclamation marks to indicate agreement.

(6) Use a highlighter for one purpose—maybe to highlight important dates or numbers.

(7) Personalize the text whenever you can.

The Internationalization of the United States

Globalization was typically associated with the expansion of American enterprise and culture to other countries, yet the United States experienced the dynamic forces of globalization within its own borders. Already in the 1980s, Japanese, European, and Middle Eastern investors had purchased American stocks and bonds, real estate, and corporations such as Firestone and 20th Century Fox. Local communities welcomed foreign capital, and states competed to recruit foreign automobile plants. American non-union workers began to produce Hondas in Marysville, Ohio, and BMWs in Spartanburg, South Carolina. By 2002, the paychecks of nearly four million American workers came from foreign-owned companies.

Globalization was transforming not just the economy but American society as well, as the United States experienced a tremendous surge of immigration, part of a worldwide trend that counted some 214 million immigrants across the globe in 2010. By 2006, the United States' 35.7 million immigrants constituted 12.4 percent of the population. The 20 million who arrived between 1980 and 2005 surpassed the previous peak immigration of the first two decades of the twentieth century and exhibited a striking difference in country of origin. Eighty-five percent of the earlier immigrants had come from Europe; by the 1980s, the vast majority came from Asia and Latin America. Consequently, immigration changed the racial and ethnic compostion of the nation. By 2004, Asian Americans numbered 13 million, while 41 million Latinos constituted — at 14 percent — the largest minority group in the nation.

The promise of economic opportunity, as always, lured immigrants to America, and the Immigration and Nationality Act of 1965 enabled them to come. Although the law set an annual limit of 270,000 immigrants, it allowed close relatives of U.S. citizens to enter above the ceiling, thus creating family migration chains. In addition, the Cold War dispersal of U.S. military and other personnel around the world enabled foreigners to learn about the nation and form relationships with citizens. Moreover, during the Cold War, U.S. immigration policy was generous to refugees from Communism, welcoming more than 800,000 Cubans after Castro's revolution in 1959 and more than 600,000 Vietnamese, Laotians, and Cambodians after the Vietnam War.

Handwritten margin notes:

1
2 — Foreigner investing & purchase in the U.S.
3
4 — ??? But were American workers also laid off?
5 — !!!
6
7 — Families from home benefitted

??? But didn't this "promise" work out for most?

Excerpted from *The American Promise: A History of the United States,* Fifth Edition, by James L. Roark et al. Copyright © 2012 by Bedford/St. Martin's. Used by permission of the publisher.

Visual Walkthrough,
continued

Take Critical Thinking Notes while You Read

A science textbook can look very different from your humanities textbook, but you'll find that you can use similar strategies to critically engage with the material. As you can see in this example from a chemistry textbook, which includes abbreviations, practice exercises, and formulas for calculating medicine doses, reading a science textbook will require you to pay attention to formulas and models as well as practice the concepts through problem sets and exercises in order to understand the information.

Reading a Science Textbook

(1) Underline main ideas and key concepts.

(2) Circle specific examples.

(3) Use a highlighter for one purpose—to highlight important calculations, formulas, and numbers.

(4) Take summarizing notes in the margins that connect aspects of class to the text for better understanding.

(5) Take time to do any practice problems while reading the text, ideally without looking at the solution first.

(6) Use question marks when you have a question or don't understand the solution or answer to the practice problems.

PRACTICE EXERCISES

23 Using the conversions on page 12, convert the following units into calories:
   a. 5.79 kcal   **b.** 48.8 J
24 How many joules are there in 2.45 cal?
25 How many joules are there in 2,720 Calories, the amount of energy the average person consumes in a day?

Dosage Calculations

For some medicines prescribed for patients, the dosage must be adjusted according to the patient's weight. This is especially true when administering medicine to children. For example, a dosage of "8.0 mg of tetracycline per kilogram body weight daily" is a dosage based on the weight of the patient. A patient's weight is often given in pounds, yet many drug handbooks give the dosage per kilogram body weight of the patient. Therefore, to calculate the correct amount of medicine to give the patient, you must first convert the patient's weight from pounds into kilograms with an English-metric conversion, using Table 1-3.

It is important to recognize that the dosage is itself a conversion factor between the mass or volume of the medicine and the weight of the patient. Whenever you see the word *per*, it means *in every* and can be expressed as a ratio or fraction where *per* represents a division operation (divided by). For example, 60 miles *per* hour can be written as the ratio 60 mi/1 hr. Similarly, a dosage of 8.0 mg *per* kg body weight can be expressed as the fraction 8.0 mg/1 kg. Hence, dosage *is* a conversion factor:

$$\frac{8 \text{ mg}}{1 \text{ kg}} \quad \text{or} \quad \frac{1 \text{ kg}}{8 \text{ mg}}$$

Dimensional analysis is used to solve dosage calculations by multiplying the patient's weight by the appropriate English-metric conversion factor and then multiplying by the dosage conversion factor, as shown in the following worked exercise.

Some common abbreviations indicating the frequency with which a medication should be administered include *q.d.* and *b.i.d.*, derived from the Latin meaning administered "daily" and "twice daily," respectively. If the medicine is prescribed for two times daily or four times daily, divide your final answer by two or four to determine how much to give the patient at each administration.

WORKED EXERCISE Dosage Calculations

1-19 Tetracycline elixir, an antibiotic, is ordered at a dosage of 8.0 mg per kilogram of body weight q.d. for a child weighing 52 lb. How many milligrams of tetracycline elixir should be given to this child daily?

Solution

Step 1: Identify the conversions. Since the dosage is given based on a patient's weight in kilograms, an English-to-metric conversion must be performed. From Table 1-3 this is 1.000 kg = 2.205 lb. The dosage itself is already a conversion factor.

Step 2: Express each conversion as two possible conversion factors. The English-to-metric conversion factors for the patient's weight are

$$\frac{1 \text{ kg}}{2.205 \text{ lb}} \quad \text{or} \quad \frac{2.205 \text{ lb}}{1 \text{ kg}}$$

The dosage *is* a conversion factor between the mass of medicine in milligrams and the weight of the patient in kilograms:

$$\frac{8.0 \text{ mg}}{1 \text{ kg}} \quad \text{or} \quad \frac{1 \text{ kg}}{8.0 \text{ mg}}$$

Use a highlighter sparingly. Students often use highlighters to call out important aspects of the text. However, if you highlight too much of the text, the highlighting will become useless because you will end up having to reread most of the material anyway. Moreover, indiscriminate highlighting reduces critical thinking because it means you're not pausing to ask questions and react meaningfully. If you love highlighters, give your highlighting a specific and limited purpose.

Take extra time to save yourself time. Although taking notes increases the amount of time you need to get through a reading, the

⑤ Questions to Answer after Completing a Reading

1. What are the most important themes or concepts?

This will help you assess whether you understood the essence of the reading. And if you don't know, you need to go back and find out.

2. What examples or significant details should I remember?

Dig deeper into the material so that you can round out the overarching themes and concepts with supporting details.

3. Is the evidence presented sound? Why or why not?

Take a step back and analyze the evidence presented to push yourself to engage in critical thinking that will increase your deep understanding.

4. Does the material contradict or support other readings or lectures? How?

Connect the reading to others in the class and to what was argued in lecture to help pick out broader course themes and main arguments.

5. Why did the instructor assign this particular reading? What's the point of the reading?

Asking why the material is important in the scheme of the course will help you determine what aspects of the reading matter most.

positive trade-off is that your comprehension and engagement with the reading will be much greater. As a result, you'll retain more of the material in the short and long term. You will find it easier to complete assignments that require use of the reading. And studying the reading for tests won't take as long because you can just study your notes, rather than rereading the entire text.

Engage in Conversations

Another way to improve the effectiveness and comprehension of your reading is to talk about the material. As you talk about how various readings have shaped your understanding, you'll engage your brain in critical thinking, figure out what you know and don't know, and learn from other perspectives.

Get Support from Classmates

Form a reading group or find a classmate who is interested in working with you, and share your questions, reactions, and synthesis of assigned texts. Try to meet once a week after class or during a meal, or schedule an online discussion at a convenient time. Engaging with the texts by discussing them with other students will benefit you because you'll be more likely to notice if you don't fully understand something in the readings. And you may be inspired to rethink your understanding of the texts, helping to deepen your comprehension.

QUICK TIP

Review Your Reading

In collaboration with other classmates, create reading review questions that ask you to recall key details from your readings. Then, quiz each other by speaking answers out loud or writing them down. If it's difficult to coordinate with others in person, share the review questions online with your classmates or do this exercise on your own for an effective way to deepen your reading comprehension.

Meet with Instructors

It's also useful to talk with your instructor about readings. Visit during office hours or spend a few minutes after class explaining what you find fascinating—or what doesn't seem to make sense. Find out why your instructor assigned the reading and whether he or she can help you make deeper connections with other class material. These discussions will further your critical thinking in meaningful ways.

If you're having trouble understanding the readings, be sure to meet with your instructor. Giving your instructor a sense of the challenges you are facing in the class will allow him or her to provide more focused assistance. And if you find that you can't get through all the readings or can't stay focused while reading, be honest about this. Your instructor might provide you with course-specific reading techniques or may refer you to academic support resources at your school for assistance.

 case study

Ken explains how he deals with college reading assignments.

> With so many assigned readings, it can be tough to prioritize. I found that the best way to stay on top of all the readings is to plan ahead. The biggest difficulty I had was time management. During my first year, I would start my readings after dinner, which would usually lead to a late night. I was very motivated and eager to get straight As, so often I would stay up until 2 a.m. or even later. I thought this is how hard you're supposed to work in college to succeed, but I could have simply worked smarter and attended class without feeling exhausted.
>
> During my second year, I broke my study sessions into blocks throughout the day. I read while I was at work or while riding a stationary bike at the gym. I did my readings anywhere I had the opportunity in order to reduce the workload later. When nighttime came around, I didn't look at my readings as a never-ending task because I had already finished most of them during the day.

Another great benefit of this habit was that I was better able to retain the information I read. When I did all my readings in one segment for several hours straight, I found that I couldn't recall the information as clearly as when I had breaks between my readings. Taking breaks helps retention because the brain can absorb only so much information before it runs out of energy. Spreading my readings throughout the day was one of the most important changes I made in college.

QUESTIONS FOR REFLECTION   Have you been able to complete readings by the due date, or do you find that you're constantly playing catch-up? If you're struggling to get through your readings, first determine the cause: Are you not giving yourself enough time? Are you distracted while you're reading? Or are you having trouble understanding the texts? Then, try a new reading strategy to address the issue for example, start readings at least three days before the due date; change your reading location; write more notes using critical thinking strategies; or seek help from your instructor and check into what academic support resources might be available at your school.

9

iStock.com/CagriOgner

Test Taking

Y our first big college exam is tomorrow. You have a good grasp of the material, but you'd like to study additional readings and class notes. Should you plan to stay up really late to finish studying? Should you also study right before the start of the exam instead of eating breakfast? Perhaps you're feeling anxious and hope you don't blank during the test, which has happened to you in the past. And what if you don't finish the exam in time? Taking tests in college can be a nerve-wracking experience. And since tests are typically given less frequently in college than in high school, they may count for more of your final grade and are higher stakes. That's why it's important to understand the strategies that will help you succeed. If you are feeling this anxiety, just know that you aren't alone and there are resources at your disposal to help you conquer your next test. This chapter addresses what you can expect before, during, and after your test and offers advice to help you perform at your best and learn from your mistakes.

LaunchPad Solo
macmillan learning

To access the LearningCurve study tool, video activities, and more, go to *LaunchPad Solo for College Success.* macmillanlearning.com/collegesuccessmedia

141

Before the Test

One of the most important things you can do before a test is to study well in advance. Plan ahead by starting your studying at least a few days, if not a full week, before the test to give yourself time to take thoughtful study notes and to ask any pressing questions. Studying in advance will help you digest the material more fully and will reduce anxiety because you won't be trying to cram every little detail into your brain the night before.

Cramming typically doesn't work for college tests because it leaves you with only a surface-level understanding rather than a deep grasp of the material. When you give your brain just a limited amount of time to learn the information, you're more likely to forget what you studied. You may also have a harder time recalling details and applying what you know to novel problems that are on the exam.

The Night before

Try to get a good night's sleep before the test. A good night's sleep varies from person to person, but most people need a six- to eight-hour block of sleep. When you're tired, your brain doesn't function as well as it does when you're rested. Lack of sleep makes it more difficult for you to remember things and to be creative, and your ability to recall information slows down—factors that can negatively affect your performance on tests.

The Morning of the Test

If you plan to finish studying the morning of the test, be careful not to cram in too much. A rushed morning will only increase your stress. Give yourself enough time to get ready, and be sure to dress in something that makes you feel comfortable—the last thing you should be thinking about is how uncomfortable you are while taking the test. If you're particularly anxious, especially on your way to the test, try using some techniques to calm yourself, such as listening to music or deep breathing.

QUICK TIP

Feed Your Mind

Take time to eat something substantial that will help you maintain your energy and focus. Tests can be quite taxing on your brain, so you need fuel to keep yourself going. And if you're allowed, bring a snack and a drink to the test in case you need a boost right before or in the middle of the exam.

© Jatson Love/CartoonStock.com

College tests usually are less frequent and cover much more material than tests in high school. But if you want to retain all you need to know, use study strategies such as planning ahead and studying over the course of several days, rather than cramming for the test the night before.

Right before the Test

Be sure to get to the test with time to spare. Arriving early means that you'll be able to find a seat that feels comfortable. Maybe you need the extra leg room at the end of a row or prefer to be near a window. Increasing your comfort level during the test will only help you. The additional time will also give you the chance to look over any final materials or your study notes and to begin focusing on the task ahead.

During and after the Test

There's a lot to think about once you start the exam. Not only are you trying to answer questions correctly, thoroughly, and thoughtfully, but you're also trying to complete the test in the time allotted. Looking over the exam, checking the clock periodically, and keeping yourself focused will help.

Look Over the Exam

As soon as you receive the exam, take a minute to quickly look over the entire exam. This strategy can help get your brain going (as it begins processing the answers to the questions) as well as help you pace yourself as you begin the test.

QUICK TIP

Conquer Online Tests

Online tests can be set up very differently than traditional tests, so while the same strategies apply, you might find you have to adjust your methods when answering questions in an online setting. Ask your instructor if you are able to interact with the testing site prior to the test so you can get more comfortable with the online testing system.

⑤ Questions To Ask Yourself after Looking Over the Exam

1. How many questions are on the exam, and how long do I have to complete it?

Skimming the entire test will give you a sense of the types of questions on the test, will jumpstart your brain to start thinking about the material, and will allow you to make an estimated guess on how long it will take to complete.

2. Where should I be halfway through the time allotted?

Determining how much of the test you should complete halfway through the time allotted will help you pace yourself during the test.

3. Are certain questions worth more than others?

Spending more time on questions that are worth more is important, given that your answers will impact your overall test grade more significantly.

4. Do I fully understand the directions?

Reading directions (and all test questions) very carefully will help you reduce mistakes that result from misunderstanding what you're being asked to do. Having points taken off your score merely for misunderstanding directions can be frustrating, especially if you knew the correct answer.

5. Are there questions I need to ask the instructor?

Don't be afraid or embarrassed to ask questions before or during the test if you are confused about directions or what's being asked on the test.

CHAPTER 9

Visual Walkthrough

Taking the Test

Once the test is handed out, don't immediately start answering the questions. Take a minute to look over the test to get a sense of what you will need to complete in the time allotted.

1. Be sure to write your name on the test.

2. Read the directions carefully to be sure you know what is expected. Then, quickly skim each page of the test to familiarize yourself with what's to come.

3. Calculate how much of the total grade each question represents. The first five short-answer questions are worth 75 percent of the grade, while the five definitions are worth 25 percent. You will want to spend more time on those questions that are worth more and try to allocate your time accordingly: for this test, you would spend about 75 percent of your time (45 minutes) on the first five questions, and the remainder of your time (15 minutes) on the definitions.

4. Note how much time you have to complete the exam so that you can figure out where you should be at specific points in the test. Since the time allotted is one hour and the start time is 11 a.m., you need to complete the five short-answer questions by 11:45 a.m. to give yourself enough time to define the five terms at the end of the test. Check the clock periodically. If you're still on question 2 at the halfway point (11:30 a.m.), you'll need to move more quickly through the remaining questions to complete the test in time.

5. Write notes on the exam to help you. For example, write down when you need to complete certain sections or how much time you should spend on specific questions.

Name _____

Psychology 101 Exam (start time 11:00 a.m.)

Directions: Answer the following five short-answer questions in as much detail as possible (each question is worth 15 points). Then, define the five terms outlined at the end of the exam (each definition is worth 5 points). You have one hour to complete the exam. Good luck! ③ ④

Short Answer Questions: (Need to finish this section by 11:45 a.m.!)

1. What are the five stages of personality development from birth to adolescence, and what defines each of these stages?

2. At what stage does a child's conscience develop, and what influences are important?

3. What are the sources of human self-esteem, according to Sigmund Freud?

4. How has Freud's model of the ego evolved over time, and what does the ego have to control?

5. What constitutes a "healthy" personality in adulthood, according to Marie Jahoda?

Define the following terms: (Spend no more than 3 minutes on each term.) ⑤

a. Epigenetic principle

b. Incorporative stage

c. Precocious conscience

d. Identity confusion

e. Distantiation

Keep Track of Time

Try to pace yourself by checking the clock periodically. It's easy to stay stuck on one problem for a long time, but this wastes valuable time. The longer you mull over a difficult question, the more anxious and frustrated you can become, blocking the free flow of thought and making it even harder to come up with your answer.

Keep moving. If you find yourself getting stuck on a question, circle that question and then move on to the next one. Your subconscious will actually still be working on the questions you skip, and you'll likely gain insight as you move to other questions. Just remember to go back to any questions you skipped to see if you can come up with good answers.

Assess your progress. Once your time is halfway up, assess where you are in the test. If you're about where you should be, keep going. If you're ahead of where you should be, keep going. If you're behind and don't know how you're ever going to answer all the remaining questions, try to shorten your answers if possible, and keep going.

Be concise. Answers to exam questions don't have to be beautifully written. When time is short, you might need to write in shorthand or use bullet points. Write as much as time allows, even if your response is not as thorough as you'd like. If you leave the question blank because time is short, your instructor might assume that you didn't know the answer at all; but if you answer the question, even briefly, your instructor will see that you've grasped aspects of the material.

Focus on You (Not on Your Classmates!)

Don't compare yourself to those around you during the test. Don't waste your valuable time and brainpower worrying that your neighbor is already on page 3 of the exam when you're still on page 1. Your neighbor may not have answered all the questions or may have a different strategy for completing the test. Whatever the case, stay focused on what you are doing. Check the time, not your peers, to help you move through the test.

> **QUICK TIP**
>
> **Check Your Work**
>
> Checking your work always pays off. Never leave an exam early. Instead, check your answers to be sure you feel confident in them. Add more detail if you can. Sometimes you'll remember something as you're going along and can add information or examples to some of your answers.

Don't Let Your Eyes Wander—Ever

Be careful not to show any signs of cheating. Keep your eyes focused on the exam or on the clock, not on your neighbor. Cheating is a very serious offense, and if instructors catch you cheating, or even suspect you of cheating, you will face severe consequences. You may fail the class, be suspended for a term or a year, or even be expelled from school.

If you feel tempted to cheat, ask yourself why. Are you struggling to understand concepts in the class and don't think you'll pass otherwise? Do you have trouble performing to your capacity on tests and don't know what else to do? Are you not studying enough to do well on the test? No matter what your reasons may be, cheating is dishonest and could severely impact your future and your relationships. Before you resort to cheating, take the time to get tutoring or help with test taking and studying. You'll be happy you did.

Getting the Test Back

Be sure to review your test when you get it back because doing so will help you improve your score the next time. Don't let a bad test score discourage you; almost every student will experience a disappointment at some point in his or her college career. It's important to learn from your mistakes and move forward. You might find that you lost points because you made careless mistakes, were rushed, or didn't check your work. Or you might discover that you need to adjust your study strategies in order to get an in-depth understanding of the material. This information is valuable; it will allow you to learn from your mistakes and lead you to implement strategies that will help you succeed the next time.

⑤ **Ways** to Learn from Your Test Mistakes

1. Check over all your answers to see what you got wrong or lost points on.

You need to know what you didn't get right so that you can study that material and understand it more deeply the next time you're tested on it.

2. Go back to the class material and figure out the correct answers.

Once you know what you got wrong, be sure to find out what the correct answer is.

3. Ask your instructor for clarification if you don't know why your answers were marked wrong.

Wondering why you got something wrong won't help you if that material comes up again on a future test. Find out why you got it wrong, and make sure you understand the instructor's explanation.

4. If you're going to be tested again on the same material you missed, be sure you fully understand it for the next test.

You don't want to be in the middle of a test and realize that you still don't understand the concept that you got wrong on the previous test.

5. If you didn't perform as well as you'd like, talk with your instructor about class-specific test preparation tips before the next exam.

Be honest with yourself and your instructor if you didn't do as well as you expected on the test, especially if you studied a lot. You might not be studying in the right way.

Q case study

Natasha shares her test-taking advice.

It is important to take advantage of all of your resources. Instructors almost always have office hours available for their students to come in and ask questions before the test, and they can usually be reached through e-mail. A couple of days before the exam, many instructors also set up a review session that is open to their students. It's important to go to those sessions and ask your instructor to clarify any confusing points about the exam or the material.

The night before the test, don't stay up late studying. Sleep and nutrition will be better for you than spending the late hours poring over your books. On test day, get up early and allow yourself time to be comfortable—and be sure to eat a good breakfast.

When you receive the test, look through it quickly after listening to or reading the directions to make sure you know how to pace yourself. It is important to gauge your time and go back over your work if you have time to spare.

Know what to expect before you arrive at the test. If you know what the exam will look like and have an idea of what type of questions will be asked, you can prepare for it. The good thing is that most instructors will help you out and will let you know what the exams are going to be like. Being proactive is what will help you the most.

QUESTIONS FOR REFLECTION What has been your experience with test taking? Have you successfully paced yourself during tests, or have you run out of time and left questions blank? If you tend to run out of time, reflect on what's happening during the test so that you can find solutions. Are you moving too slowly through the test because you lose track of time or get stuck on questions? Are you dealing with test anxiety? Use the strategies discussed in this chapter to address any test issues you're facing. If you continue to struggle, seek help from an Academic Advising Office.

Managing Test Anxiety

Exams in college can feel quite weighty since they often count for a significant part of your grade. And because just a few tests are given in most college classes, each test score has a big impact on your final grade in the class. Given these factors, it's normal to experience test anxiety. Fortunately, you can use a variety of strategies that reduce this anxiety before and during the exam.

Practice, Practice, Practice

If you play an instrument or play on a sports team, you know that your skill and comfort level improve the more you practice. The same benefits of practice apply to test taking. The more you practice and

© Theresa McCracken/CartoonStock.com

Unfortunately, there is no magic ball that will tell you exactly what will be on the test. However, by practicing and becoming more familiar with various testing situations, you'll start to feel more at ease when taking exams during college.

put yourself in testing situations, the easier test taking becomes. So, take practice tests that have the same types of questions as an upcoming test, and put yourself in situations that mimic the surroundings and time frame of the test. Becoming more familiar with something puts you at ease—a good starting point before taking an exam.

Reduce Your Stress

Do everything you can to reduce your stress the day of the test. We discussed some of these techniques earlier in the chapter: Arrive at the test early so that you can find a good seat. Wear clothing that makes you feel comfortable. Eat something nutritious that will maintain your energy during the test.

And finally, another key to reducing test anxiety is to avoid classmates who are anxious or overly negative. Your anxiety will only increase if you listen to comments such as "This test is going to be impossible" or "I'm so worried" or "I bet there will be tons of trick questions." Steer clear of these types of negative exchanges before the test.

If You Blank

Students sometimes freeze while taking a test. Their hearts start racing, their minds go blank, and they can't remember the information they need to answer the questions. If you blank, try not to panic. Instead, take steps to calm yourself and alter your state of mind. The strategies in the following checklist will help you regain your composure and get back on track.

Once you feel calmer, slowly reread the question or problem you're stuck on, and freewrite for a few minutes just to get you going. Write whatever comes into your head. Don't worry about what it sounds like. Just write down what you know. Then, go back and work through as much of the problem as you can, using your freewriting as a guide. Your answer may not be perfect, but giving an imperfect answer is better than leaving the question blank.

And if you still can't answer the question, skip it. Move on to an easier question that you *can* answer. Working on other questions may jog your memory so that later you can go back and answer the questions you skipped.

When to Get Help

Blanking on a test is frightening. Feelings of anxiety can take over, making it difficult to write coherent answers to questions or to complete portions of the test. If you try the techniques discussed in this chapter and they don't help, something more may be going on. For example, you may not be studying in the most effective way. Or stresses in your personal life may be affecting your academic life.

Whatever the case, be sure to seek out help whenever you experience severe test anxiety. Go to your advisor, your instructor, your teaching assistant, your mentor, or someone at the Academic Advising Office, and explain what happens to you when you take a test. One of these people will be able to give you the support you need. Remember: you're never alone in these situations. The more you try to hide your anxiety, the worse it will get. Your college success depends on seeking help when you need it.

✓ Checklist for Reducing Test Anxiety

○ Take several deep breaths. Continue for a few minutes until you get your breathing and heart rate under control.

○ Tense and then relax different muscle groups. Move your shoulders in circles, massage your lower back, and move your feet around to get blood flowing.

○ Think of positive images to reduce your anxiety. Picture a scene you find peaceful, and think about what you see, hear, feel, and smell.

○ Eat or drink something satisfying that will make you feel better.

○ Use positive self-talk to help you cope and move you forward. For example, repeat, "I have the ability to do this," *not* "I'm going to fail this test."

○ Think briefly about post-exam rewards. What fun will you have after the exam is over?

10

Writing and Information Literacy

iStock.com/CagriOgner

Writing in college can feel a bit overwhelming, especially during your first year. The expectations of your college instructors will likely be different from those of your high school teachers, and the assignments may be longer and more challenging. Maybe you have never written a lengthy research paper before. Or maybe you find yourself asking: what's the difference between MLA and APA citations? And sometimes you may feel stuck and not know where to start on your ten-page assignment. But if you plan ahead, incorporate critical thinking, and ask for feedback, you will be able to tackle papers with ease while also improving your writing skills. College is also a time during which you'll engage in research, evaluate both online and print sources, learn how to use technology and the library to access resources, and also communicate with your peers and instructors in a professional manner. These are all important skills to master along your college journey.

LaunchPad Solo
macmillan learning

To access the LearningCurve study tool, video activities, and more, go to *LaunchPad Solo for College Success.* macmillanlearning.com/collegesuccessmedia

155

General Writing Advice

Don't be surprised if you get lower grades on your first college papers or a greater amount of constructive criticism than you're used to. Remember that writing is a process and that you can improve your writing with practice and hard work. Get started on the right track by keeping the following suggestions in mind.

Understand the Assignment

Take the time to fully understand the paper assignment and expectations. Although writing is a personal process, you do have to answer the question that's being asked. Your instructor will grade your paper based on his or her perspective and expectations, so meet with your instructor well in advance of the due date to be sure you're interpreting the assignment properly. And be honest with your instructor if this is the first time you've encountered a particular type of writing assignment. Ask to see an example of a solid, well-written paper. In addition, find out if your instructor has any course-specific writing strategies or advice to make the process go more smoothly for you.

Write Rough Drafts and Obtain Feedback

Plan ahead by writing a rough draft of your paper a few days—or, better yet, a week—before it's due. To craft a well-written paper, you need to write a few drafts before you submit the final paper. Writing a draft will reduce your paper-writing stress in a couple of ways: it will ease you into writing the final product, and because you're planning ahead, it will prevent you from experiencing extreme time pressure when writing. Help yourself follow through with the drafting process by using your planner to determine when you'll start and finish your draft.

Be sure to complete the rough draft by the deadline you set so that you have time to edit the draft and, even more importantly, time to ask someone else to provide comments. Try to schedule time for

© Fran/CartoonStock.com

It is important to make sure you have enough time before an assignment is due in order to revise your first draft. Getting a rough draft of your ideas is an important step in the writing process. Through drafting, feedback, and revision, you'll be able to polish your writing to the level it needs to be in order to submit to your instructor.

your instructor, a writing tutor, or a trusted peer to read your rough draft before you hand the paper in. Another perspective and a second pair of eyes will help you see where evidence is missing, where your writing is too wordy, where your argument can be fine-tuned, and where your sentences and word choice can be improved. Don't hesitate to ask for assistance, and then act upon your reader's suggestions to improve your draft.

QUICK TIP

Visit a **Writing Center**

Taking advantage of a writing center or similar resource will ensure that your papers are well developed and that you're getting a fresh perspective on your writing. Writing tutors and advisors can assist you with all aspects of your paper, including the presentation of your argument and conclusions, the structure, grammar, and even brainstorming a paper topic.

⑤ **Ways** to Improve Your Papers

1. **Write an introduction that draws your reader in.**

    An introduction sets the scene for the rest of the paper and draws a reader in. If it's good, your readers' first impressions will be positive. If it's not good, readers might view the rest of the paper in a more negative light.

2. **Vary sentence length to make the paper more interesting.**

    Too many long sentences can be boring, and too many short sentences can feel choppy. Variety helps keep the reader engaged.

3. **Don't use too many quotations from your sources; instead, interpret your sources in an interesting way.**

    Instructors want to see your own critical thinking. So quote sparingly, and spend time interpreting your sources.

4. **Don't spend the entire conclusion of your essay summarizing your argument; instead, add a new insight that your reader will remember.**

    Leave the reader with something to think about, rather than a mere summary of the previous pages.

5. **Be sure to edit, edit, edit!**

    Instructors may give you a lower grade on your paper if they find careless errors. So take the time to carefully edit and proofread your paper.

Apply Critical Thinking

Writing papers requires thinking, especially critical thinking. When you're completing writing assignments, be sure to apply the five steps for critical thinking. Following these steps will deepen your thinking when you tackle your writing assignments.

Step 1: Ask Questions

Before you begin writing, ask yourself what you need to include in the paper both to answer the question and to meet your instructor's expectations. What topics could you write about, and which ones seem more interesting or more plausible? If you need to incorporate class readings into the paper, which ones are most relevant, and why? If you want to prove an argument, what evidence and examples do you need to provide in order to produce a strong paper? The more questions you ask and answer in advance, the more you're thinking critically about the paper.

Step 2: Evaluate Your Reactions

Evaluate your reactions to the assignment and to your research, and allow these reactions to guide how you will approach the paper. Let's say you need to incorporate two readings into your writing assignment, and you disagree with both authors. Use this reaction to inspire the core of the paper, in which you might thoughtfully present counterarguments to the two authors' arguments.

Or if you're writing a laboratory report for a science class and your results don't conform with what the course textbook leads you to expect, you could analyze why you think this is the case. This type of analysis shows that you've thought carefully about the information presented.

Step 3: Write with a "Critical Lens"

Consider how you can incorporate novel insights into your paper. In your readings, have you found any holes in the arguments? Has any evidence been skewed or ignored? In your paper, demonstrate that you have thoughtfully considered several perspectives, and explain why you believe each argument is or is not clearly articulated and supported. This type of thinking will demonstrate that you're not taking everything you're learning at face value; instead, you are critically analyzing material in a meaningful way.

Step 4: Make Connections

By making meaningful connections between various aspects of the class in your paper—for example, by exploring how the lectures connect to the readings—you can examine the big picture without losing sight of important details. Synthesizing all the course material could reveal important insights and may push your thinking to a deeper level, improving the paper.

Step 5: Bring Your Experiences into the Assignment

Bringing "you" into your papers may not work in some subjects, but in others it can shape your thinking and make a paper more interesting and meaningful. Let's say you're completing a paper in a political science class and you realize that your involvement in a political campaign offers useful insights. Try to incorporate this experience into your paper—doing so can deepen your argument and help you answer the question in a unique way.

Getting Started: The Writing Process

Some students love to write papers; others dread the writing process. But almost all students will face writing situations in which they struggle to pick a topic, have difficulty developing an argument, or just can't seem to get started. For many college students, the writing process feels overwhelming, especially at the beginning when they're staring at a blank page. So if you're feeling some anxiety at the thought of writing a paper, you're not alone. The following strategies can help reduce that anxiety and get you started.

Before You Start Writing

Before you begin writing the paper, you can do a number of things to help you focus on the task ahead and get underway. Knowing how to get the writing process started will also keep you calm.

Figure out how to make the topic interesting or relevant. Writing about something you find interesting makes the writing process much easier and more engaging. While this can sometimes be difficult because you do have to work within the parameters of the assignment, by all means talk to an instructor, a writing tutor, or a peer if you struggle. Brainstorming possible ideas may help you come up with a meaningful connection you hadn't thought of alone, and that could inspire your paper writing in an important way.

Establish your argument. Start by figuring out your main argument. Then, write a one- or two-sentence thesis that lays out what you plan to argue in the paper. Writing a thesis is important because it's the blueprint of your paper—it tells the reader what your argument is and how you plan to prove it. To develop a thesis, think about why the topic interested you in the first place. What made it compelling, and why? Can you clearly articulate a meaningful argument about this topic? Can you support your argument with evidence?

Write a thorough outline. Writing an outline allows you to add detail to your thesis and determine the structure of the paper without worrying about making the prose beautiful. Writing an outline jumpstarts the thinking process so that you can begin to figure out the argument and supporting evidence for your paper. An outline gives clear direction to your writing, making the writing process feel more manageable and reducing your anxiety about writing. A completed outline is also reassuring because you can see that you do, in fact, have something to say about a particular topic.

Take time to freewrite. If you're stuck and can't get going, take some time to freewrite about the topic. Remember: the first draft of your paper doesn't have to be perfect. In fact, it shouldn't be. You will stifle your own writing if you put too much pressure on yourself to get the first draft exactly right. To get your juices flowing, just start typing words on the screen that are in some way related to your topic and thesis.

QUICK TIP

Make Freewriting a Conversation

When you freewrite, pretend that you're talking to someone about the topic you picked. What's on your mind? What do you want to say? What are you hoping to prove or disprove? Why is the topic important to you? This technique will help you articulate your argument more clearly.

While You're Writing

You can take some steps *during* the paper-writing process to reduce any anxiety you may have. The following strategies will make the writing process feel more manageable, will help you write in your own voice, and will show you how to write more effectively and efficiently.

Break it down. Don't focus on writing the entire paper in one sitting, which can feel overwhelming and make it difficult to begin. Instead, break up the paper into smaller tasks, and build in refreshing breaks to keep you energized. For example, complete the first paragraph, and then take a ten-minute break. Tackle the next two paragraphs, and take another short break. The more you can break down the writing process into smaller chunks, the easier it will be to fill those blank pages.

Write in your own voice. Your instructor wants to see *your* voice, thoughts, and arguments in a paper, not your classmates' or your teaching assistant's ideas. If you use words that you barely understand or write phrases that sound false, the paper will not ring true for anyone, including you.

Read your writing aloud. To check whether your writing makes sense, is articulated clearly, and sounds like you, read it out loud. Do this regularly throughout the writing process. If a phrase or a sentence doesn't sound right, rework it so that you like what you hear. If you're stuck writing a paragraph, read what you have written out loud, and then keep talking to see if you can clearly state what you're trying to say. Also read aloud for friends or others to test your writing. It may be a little scary to read your writing in front of other people, but ask for their honest feedback—it will improve your writing.

 ## case study

Yen shares her thoughts on how to get started on college writing assignments.

I found that starting my papers was the most challenging part of the writing process. I wanted my first draft to be just right, so it was often hard to get going. I felt almost paralyzed with fear staring at a blank page. And I also felt overwhelmed, given the length of the papers I had to turn in and the intense thinking required. After getting some low paper grades back, I finally ended up going to my college's writing center and talked to a tutor who happened to be an upperclassman and had faced similar challenges as a first-year student.

After talking with her, I realized that I was better off writing a thorough outline to start my papers and to set early deadlines for myself to motivate me to start a paper at least a week or more in advance. By starting earlier and referencing a well thought out outline, I found papers became easier to start, and since I was only writing a rough draft, I didn't feel as much pressure to make every sentence perfect the first time around.

QUESTIONS FOR REFLECTION What has been your experience so far with writing papers? Do you find it difficult to start writing? If so, how do you get yourself going? If you procrastinate and wait until the last minute, consider connecting with writing resources on campus to help motivate you to write a rough draft in advance.

✅ **Checklist for Starting the Writing Process**

- ⭕ Pick a paper topic that interests you.
- ⭕ Figure out your main argument and write a thesis.
- ⭕ Write a thorough outline of the paper.
- ⭕ Freewrite to get started.
- ⭕ Break the paper into smaller chunks.
- ⭕ Take breaks frequently.
- ⭕ Write in your own voice.
- ⭕ Read your writing out loud.

Avoiding Plagiarism

Whenever you use research in a college paper, you must cite the source of this research. You must also give credit to authors or anyone else if you include their ideas in your paper. Always cite the source of any words or ideas that are not your own, including research you find on Internet sites.

Citing Your Sources

If you fail to give credit to your sources, you are plagiarizing. Plagiarizing is using other people's words or ideas without revealing where they came from. You must cite your sources not only when you quote someone else's words but also when you use someone else's arguments, evidence, or ideas. If you're caught plagiarizing, even if you claim that you weren't aware of any wrongdoing or thought you were citing properly, you can get into serious trouble—from failing the course to being expelled. Plagiarism is a serious offense, so you must take it seriously.

QUICK TIP

Understand Your College's Code of Conduct

Most colleges have a code of conduct that explicitly defines plagiarism, outlines expectations for academic honesty, and lists the consequences for breaking those rules. Familiarize yourself with this code of conduct so that you know exactly what your college expects of students.

Cite your sources as you write. As you're writing a paper that uses sources, cite your sources whenever you use quotations in your paper or incorporate any ideas that are not your own. It's important to cite your sources as you write—otherwise, you might forget which words and ideas are your own and which come from your sources. Take the time to put the author's name and page number in parentheses after a quotation or at the end of a sentence if you include someone else's words or thoughts.

Keep your sources sorted throughout your writing process. Papers that require multiple sources, such as research papers, can be especially challenging because you have to keep track of many sources at once. To ensure that you are citing all sources properly during the brainstorming, outlining, and actual writing of your paper, start by going through each of your sources and typing out relevant quotations or ideas you'd like to incorporate in your paper, along with citations for each source. That way, you can refer to this "source document" you've created with proper citations rather than having to constantly go back to the multiple sources you're using to find what you're looking for.

QUICK TIP

Cite Class Notes Properly

If you use your class notes to inform your paper writing, be sure to give credit to your instructor and any teaching assistants if the ideas you are incorporating are theirs and not your own. Similarly, you'll need to cite classmates or class discussions to give proper credit where credit is due.

Use an Accepted Citation Style

Not all classes will follow the same citation guidelines, but all instructors will expect you to cite your sources, including sources you find on the Internet. Usually, a course syllabus details the preferred citation style for the class; if not, be sure to ask your instructor. Humanities courses often use MLA (Modern Language Association) style or *The Chicago Manual of Style*, while science and social science courses usually use APA (American Psychological Association) style or a style guide geared for engineering or science writing. Make sure

© Grizelda/CartoonStock.com

It's fine to quote sources in your paper, as long as you cite those sources properly. But if your paper is filled with other writers' ideas and you're having trouble writing in your own words, get help from your instructor or a writing center. Don't hand in a paper whose words and ideas come mostly (or solely!) from another source. College instructors expect you to write papers that show your own critical thinking.

you know what citation style each instructor expects you to use, and have the appropriate style guide with you when you are working on assignments so that you can refer to it regularly.

Researching and Communicating in a Digital Age

Technology has transformed the way we perform research and the way we communicate. The Internet has increased the amount of information flowing between people. All sorts of resources are now available online, including journal articles, newspapers, documentaries, dictionaries, maps, photographs, and videos. Resources that formerly existed only in hard copy, including entire books, are now online. Anyone can post information in the form of blogs, Wikipedia entries, or personal Web sites, even if they aren't experts, and using social media to stay connected is an essential part of our day-to-day digital interactions.

Navigating the World of Research Technology

The Internet provides powerful online research tools. In college, you'll be asked to use research in writing assignments, projects, and class discussions, so you need to know how to conduct research on the Internet appropriately. Not all information you find on the Internet is trustworthy. You need to know how to determine which sources are credible and which are not.

Evaluate online sources.   Google is a powerful tool, but use it wisely. Using search engines to find information can be a good starting point, but you must evaluate the results carefully. Many online sources of data haven't been vetted by experts in a field, so it's sometimes difficult to know whether the information you find is accurate or credible. For example, your instructor might not allow you to use research found on Wikipedia, a widely used online encyclopedia. Wikipedia articles are written collaboratively by volunteers and can be edited by anyone, so the information presented may or may not be accurate, depending on how knowledgeable the authors are about the topic.

Assess Web site credibility. One way to quickly assess the credibility of a Web site is to check the domain extension, or the last letters of the site, such as .com, .org, .gov, or .edu. A Web site address ending in .com usually indicates a commercial or business site. Most of these sites are trying to sell something and want to shed a positive light on the product being promoted, so alternative views usually are not represented. If the Web site address ends in .org, the site is usually sponsored by an organization or a not-for-profit association that is offering credible information. But information presented on .org sites might be biased, depending on the Web site sponsor. Web sites with addresses ending in .gov or .edu are considered the most credible because the information provided on the sites comes from the federal government or from educational institutions.

---

⑤ Questions to Ask When Evaluating Online Sources

1. What is the actual source of the information?

In other words, who is the author of the material, and does the person or group have relevant credentials and expertise?

2. Are other references cited in the material?

Check what references are cited when you use Internet material so that you understand what original sources influenced the information being presented.

3. Does my instructor and/or a reference librarian consider this a credible online source?

If you want to use research from the Internet and are uncertain about its quality, check with your instructor or a reference librarian before you use it.

4. Who is sponsoring the site or information presented?

Determine if the material might be biased depending on who or what organization is posting or backing the Web site.

5. Is there a more credible source I could use?

If you are in doubt, talk to your instructor and a reference librarian about which Internet sources are acceptable to use in your paper and which are not.

Using Electronic Resources at the Library

College library Web sites provide a number of electronic resources. You'll find research tools that connect you to millions of journal articles as well as newspapers, books, archived information, and more. Take the time to explore what electronic resources the library offers—especially because those sources are likely to be credible—and to learn how to navigate your library's online system.

Librarians are a trusted resource. Be sure to speak with a reference librarian, who can assist you as you navigate your library's electronic research databases. Library staff not only can save you time but can also point you in the right direction if you're not sure where to start your research.

Don't forget about printed books. We often rely on computers to do research, but don't forget to look at the printed books in your college library. Although your library may have many digitized books online, you might find good sources for your assignment in the pages of a printed book. So take the time to browse the library's shelves.

Communicating Effectively

The Internet will be an integral part of your academic life in college, as just described, and is also an integral way you will communicate with all those in your college circles. Recognize that you need to keep your audience in mind when you are sending digital communication, whether via texts, e-mails, or online discussion boards. The way you send messages to your peers will likely differ from the way you send messages to your instructors, a college staff member, or your mentor. And it's important to recognize the times that it is more effective (and much easier) *not* to use technology to communicate your message.

Recognize when to use your technology and when to use your own voice. It can be easy to hide behind our phones and computers, especially when communicating with those in authority or others we don't know well, or when we are in new and challenging situations. And while there are of course benefits to sending an e-mail or a text, often you'll be better off if you set up an in-person meeting or pick up the phone, especially if you are trying to resolve a conflict or need to discuss an obstacle you are currently facing.

CHAPTER 10

Visual Walkthrough

Send Professional E-mails

E-mail is an essential communication method in college. And while it's OK to send casual e-mails to your peers you know well, your e-mails to instructors, mentors, and other college staff members should be both professional and well written. Remember to always reread your e-mails before sending them, too! This sample e-mail to an instructor will show you how to structure your own e-mails.

(1) Use the subject line to clearly detail why you are writing the e-mail so the recipient has a sense of what's to come in the body of the e-mail.

(2) It's polite to start with a greeting and to share who you are in case the recipient may need a reminder.

(3) Using full sentences, explain succinctly why you are writing and what you are requesting.

(4) Be specific when you are asking for something and offer suggestions to try to reduce the number of e-mails you'll need to send back and forth.

(5) Always end with a salutation as a show of respect and professionalism.

File Message Insert Options Format Text Review Adobe PDF

Calibri (Body) · 14 · A˙ A˙ | Attach File ⚑ Follow Up ·
B *I* U ☰ · ☰ · ⪪ ⪫ Attach Item · ! High Importance
Paste Names
⟍ · A · ☰ ☰ ☰ Signature · ⬇ Low Importance Zoom
Clipboard Basic Text Include Tags Zoom

MailTips could not be retrieved.

From · James.Smith@schoolmail.edu

Send To... Susan.Strong@schoolmail.edu

Cc...

Bcc...

① Subject: Biology 101: Question regarding confusing results from gene expression lab-James Smith

Dear Professor Strong,

② Good afternoon. I am a student in your Biology 101 class this semester, and I have been analyzing results from our recent gene expression lab. It seems that our group's findings are at odds with ③ the rest of the class, and after referring back to lecture notes, as well as relevant class readings, I am having a difficult time explaining why that may have happened. I would like to discuss this with you in order to gain your insight as to what might have happened during the lab and how to think about approaching the lab write-up due early next week.

I just tried to sign up for your office hours online, but each available slot is already booked. Given that our lab write-up is due early next week, could we schedule a time to meet that is outside ④ your office hours, probably for 20-30 minutes? I am available Wednesday morning until noon, Thursday afternoon from 2-5 p.m., and Friday anytime. I could meet you in your office, or if there is a more convenient location on campus, please let me know.

⑤ Thank you in advance for your time,
James Smith

Communicating face-to-face allows for a more authentic connection and an easier time fully understanding each other (since tone can be lost in digital communication), and often results in a more meaningful and effective/helpful dialogue. Nevertheless, some people will let you know that they much prefer communicating digitally, and for those individuals, e-mails or texts are the way to go.

Use thoughtful communication in online courses. Online courses are built on digital communication, so you need to be extra careful to thoughtfully prepare and review your posts. Before sending, think about the tone of your online communication and consider how readers could interpret—or misinterpret—what you've written. Also, don't fall into the trap that just because you are communicating digitally, you can chat with your peers as you would on social media. Be sure to write in complete sentences and use formal language in your online discussions and writing assignments, just like you would in a regular in-person class.

Stay connected through social media and also recognize when it's interfering. Social media is obviously a great way to stay connected. And it can be a great academic tool to connect with peers and instructors about course work. But recognize that social media can also be a distraction and interfere with your course work, negatively affecting your grades and overall college performance. Pay attention to any signs that your online social activity is making it less possible for you to stay focused and concentrate. If you find that you are spending too much time connecting with your friends online, consider blocking out specific times in your day to check social media and removing temptations to check social media during your study times.

part

III

Skills for Success

12

iStock.com/CagriOgner

Managing Your Money

Managing your money is one of the many responsibilities you'll have as a college student and one of the most important life skills you can develop. You may already have experience with managing a budget, a bank account, and credit cards, or college might be the first time you're dealing with your own finances. You'll have to make a number of decisions: Should you get a credit card? If you do decide on a credit card, what's the best one for you to choose? Financial aid is necessary for most college students and can get complicated. What are your sources of aid? Do you understand the interest rates and repayment plans? Are there academic expectations or obligations that go along with your aid? Whether it is your first time managing your own money or you have previous experience in this area, learning how to create and manage a budget, understand your financial aid, and use a credit card will help to ensure your long-term financial health.

LaunchPad Solo
macmillan learning

To access the LearningCurve study tool, video activities, and more, go to *LaunchPad Solo for College Success.* macmillanlearning.com/collegesuccessmedia

193

Create and Manage a Budget

The first step when managing your money in college is assessing your overall financial situation. Start by determining your sources of income. Do you have money saved for college? Are you receiving financial aid in the form of loans, stipends, or scholarships? Are you currently working, or do you plan to get a job while in school? Estimate how much money you will receive each week or each month from all of these sources. Next, calculate the expenses you'll likely have throughout the year—books, food, rent or housing, commuting, clothes, activities, and so on.

Once you have determined this information, create a grid that breaks down the term into blocks of time (weekly or monthly). Then, put together a simple budget that lists how much money you have

"WE'RE GOING TO HAVE TO CUT BACK— THESE SINGING LESSONS FOR THE KIDS, FOR INSTANCE."

© Jorodo/CartoonStock.com

Bills are an unpleasant fact of life. Be sure to account for the payment of bills such as rent, electric and gas, insurance payments, and so on in your budget. If you find that you need to adjust your budget to pay your bills, don't despair. Look for small ways to cut back on your expenses. Saving a little here and there can add up to make a huge difference.

saved, how much money you will receive and expect to earn, and your estimated expenses.

Keeping track of your expenses may sound simple, but it's easy to lose track of what you're spending when you're busy with classes, studying, a job, and various other commitments. Make it a priority to determine a budgeting system that works for you. To stay within your budget, do you need to review it every week? Or can you manage by checking your budget just once a month? Whatever system you prefer, add it to your calendar so that your budget doesn't get lost in the shuffle.

⑤ **Ways** to Track Your Expenses

1. Keep all receipts, and track your expenses at the end each week.

Weekly tracking will ensure that you know where your money is going.

2. Monitor your bank account online, daily or weekly.

Looking at your account regularly will keep your finances fresh in your mind and will help you track how your expenses are affecting your bottom line.

3. Keep track of your daily purchases on your phone, tablet, or a simple pad of paper.

By practicing this technique, you will remember all the purchases you made.

4. Add expenses to your budget as they occur.

Writing down expenses in your budget is a good way to control your spending.

5. Consider using only cash. Give yourself an allowance each week, and keep track of it. When you run low on cash, curb your spending.

Using only cash helps to control your finances because you'll know when you need to reduce your spending.

Visual Walkthrough

Budgeting

The following example of a monthly budget lists income and expenses by category. Feel free to format your budget in any way that works for you. You might want to break the budget down into weeks or to create a budget for a term or the whole academic year. You may not need to use all the categories shown in the example, or you may need to add some categories. The more you personalize the budget, the more likely you'll be to use it.

1. List all the sources of your income for each month. Include any income from a job (part-time, full-time, internship); savings; loans; and grants, scholarships, or stipend payments. Your financial aid statement may provide aid information for an entire term, so you need to calculate the amount of your aid for each month. Talk to a financial aid officer if you need help with this.

2. List your budgeted estimate for both income and expenses. Try to keep your expenses lower than your income so that you live within your means and don't run out of money or go into debt.

3. Keep track of your actual income and expenses. For example, if your job hours increase, so will your job income. And keeping track of your actual expenses will help you stay within your budget. If you have to pay more for books or utilities than you expected, you might need to cut down on entertainment or clothing purchases to stay within your budget.

4. For each month, list the nature of your expenses, including tuition, household items, phone, food, transportation, child care, books, supplies, entertainment, and other miscellaneous items you'll need.

5. Break down broad expense categories into more specific items so that you know exactly where your money goes.

6. To fully understand your financial situation each month, total up your expenses and compare your expenses to your total income. If you're struggling to live within your means, you have to either cut back on spending or find some way to increase your income. Talk to a financial aid officer or college mentor if you need assistance.

	Budgeted Amount	Actual Amount
① Sources of Income		
Job(s)		
Savings		
Loans		
Grants/scholarships		
Other		
Total Income		
④ Expenses		
Tuition		
⑤ Household		
Rent/mortgage/room and board		
Utilities (electricity, gas, cable, Internet)		
Child care		
Health care		
Cell phone		
Food		
Groceries or college meal plan		
Eating out		
Transportation		
Car payment and insurance		
Gas and repairs		
Bus/subway pass		
Books and supplies		
Entertainment		
Movies		
Concerts		
Campus events		
Miscellaneous		
Clothing		
Household products		
Other (travel, gifts, etc.)		
⑥ Total Expenses		

Understand Your Financial Aid Package

A critical piece of your financial situation is your financial aid package. You may have received a combination of federal loans, grants, scholarships, stipends, and work-study to help with tuition and other expenses. If you have any questions about your financial aid in the short or long term, meet with your financial aid officer as soon as possible to be sure you fully understand your aid package.

Types of Aid

Your financial aid package may include various types of aid, such as aid from your college, from the state government or the federal government, and from nonprofit and private organizations. Take time to understand each line item on your financial aid statement, which might include any of the following categories of aid.

Loans. A number of loan options, including private loans and federal loans, are available to help pay for college. A loan is money that you borrow and will eventually have to pay back with interest. Let's look a little more closely at each type of loan.

- Private loans come from a lender such as a bank or credit union. Private loans sometimes have variable interest rates, meaning that the rate can rise and fall, depending on the terms of the loan; variable interest rates create more uncertainty as to your future payments. The cost of a private loan may also depend on your

---

QUICK TIP

Understand Interest Rates

Be sure you fully understand what your interest rate is on any loans you have, when the interest will begin to accrue on the loan, and how much additional cost the interest will add to your loan over time. Recognize that a high interest rate can add substantial cost to your loan over time, making it take longer to pay off.

credit score and other factors, and you may not be able to get a private loan without an established credit history.

- Federal loans have a fixed interest rate that is usually lower than private loan interest rates and do not require a credit history (except for PLUS Loans). They can actually help you develop a good credit history if you manage your payments well. Federal loans include:
  - Direct Subsidized Loans (for students with financial need)
  - Direct Unsubsidized Loans (for students with no requirements to demonstrate need)
  - PLUS Loans (for parents of dependent students to help pay education expenses)
  - Federal Perkins Loans (for students with exceptional financial need)

QUICK TIP

Loan Repayment Plans

Federal and private loans have different repayment plans. You do not need to repay federal loans until after you graduate, leave school, or enroll less than half time. However, you usually have to repay private loans while you are still in school, and you have to pay all the interest that accrues during college (and thereafter). By contrast, if you have a federal *subsidized* loan, the government, not you, pays the interest that accrues during college.

Grants. Grant money is aid that is given to you to help cover the cost of college and does not need to be repaid. Many types of grants are available, and they can come from the federal government, the state government, your college or university, and public and private organizations. Federal Pell Grants are awarded to students who demonstrate financial need, and grants from your college also are usually based on financial need.

Scholarships. A scholarship, like a grant, is money that you do not need to pay back. Scholarships are awarded to students based on various criteria that reflect the values or priorities of the awarding body. Colleges, as well as high schools and state governments, often award merit scholarships based on high achievement. Some organizations offer scholarships with eligibility requirements such as race, ethnicity, religion, college major, or location. Online, you can find a variety of college scholarships by Googling "college scholarships." Although the sheer number of scholarships available might feel overwhelming, make the effort to apply—you might be able to find additional money to help defray the cost of college.

---

⑤ Questions to Ask to Ensure You Understand Your Financial Aid

1. Did I receive any scholarship money or grants that will reduce my college costs, and if so, are they likely to be offered in subsequent years?

Subtracting scholarship and grants from the total cost of college will give you a sense of what your actual cost will be that year and in future years to help with budgeting.

2. What type of loans do I have, and when will I need to start paying them back?

Know what loans you have, how much money each loan is for, what the interest terms are, and when you are expected to start paying the loans back.

3. How much will I or my family need to pay each term or year to remain in school?

You and your family will need to budget for any college payments you have throughout the year.

4. Am I expected to earn a certain amount of money each summer to contribute to my educational expenses?

Many colleges include a summer earnings expectation in financial aid packages, which is an amount of money they expect you will earn during the summer to contribute to the following year's academic expenses.

5. Am I eligible for work-study, and how much am I expected/able to earn each term under this program?

Understand how and when you need to apply for work-study jobs to ensure you are earning what is expected each term as part of your aid package.

Work-study. If you can demonstrate financial need, you might be eligible for federal work-study jobs that provide part-time work opportunities that help cover the cost of college. Schools that participate in the Federal Work-Study Program offer work-study jobs that can be on or off campus, depending on how the school administers the program. Work-study jobs are often related to a student's course of study and community service work.

Stipends. Some students receive a stipend, or an "award," which is usually a one-time payment to help offset the cost of attending college. Besides tuition, college students have additional expenses such as food, clothes, and transportation; to help students pay for these expenses, some colleges include stipends in financial aid packages, usually for students with financial need. Stipends can reduce the hours you might otherwise need to work to make ends meet.

Applying for Aid

To help your school determine what your financial aid package will include, you need to complete financial aid applications. Colleges will ask you to fill out the Free Application for Federal Student Aid (FAFSA); some colleges will also ask you to fill out the College Scholarship Service (CSS) Profile. Even if you don't think you will receive financial aid, be sure to fill out all the aid applications so that your school has a complete picture of your financial situation and can award appropriate levels of loans, grants, and scholarships.

Fill out the FAFSA. To be eligible for federal grants, loans, and work-study, you must fill out the FAFSA. This free application provides necessary financial information about you and your family that gives the college a clear idea of your ability to pay. Based on the cost of attending the school and the information you provide on the FAFSA, the college will determine how much money you receive in grants and scholarships, how much money you can borrow, and how much work-study you are eligible for. The FAFSA Web site (www .fafsa.ed.gov) provides more detailed information, including FAFSA deadlines, options for filing the FAFSA, and how to create a FAFSA pin that will allow you to sign your forms online.

Complete a CSS Profile. You can find the CSS Profile, another financial aid form, on the College Board Web site (http://student .collegeboard.org/css-financial-aid-profile). More than 350 schools require students to submit the CSS Profile when they apply for financial aid. There is a fee for submitting a CSS Profile, but the fee is waived for students with financial need. The CSS Profile gathers additional financial information, more detailed than the FAFSA, to help colleges award institutional aid, including grants, scholarships, and loans.

Reapply each year. You need to reapply for financial aid every year that you attend college, so be aware of your college's financial aid application deadlines. Applying for aid each year is necessary because your financial aid package might need to be modified if your financial situation has changed, and colleges might need to alter the financial aid they can offer, depending on changing institutional priorities or realities.

QUICK TIP

Manage Your Aid

Your financial aid package will probably change from year to year, so be sure to meet with a financial aid officer to discuss any changes in your financial situation or any questions you have.

Use Credit Cards Wisely

The decision to obtain a credit card is an important one. As soon as you open a credit card account, you start building a credit history, which is a good thing if you use the card wisely. All too often, though, credit cards tempt people to live beyond their means and to rack up debt that will negatively affect their credit score (and bank account). Because of the possible risks of using credit cards, you need to be fully informed before you decide to obtain one.

Choosing a Credit Card

Look for a credit card with no annual fee. Find out exactly how much interest will be charged if you do not pay your balance in full each month. Be aware of when interest starts accruing—it should accrue only if you do not pay the full balance on your monthly statement, not as soon as you make purchases. Credit cards often charge fees for missed or late payments, so know when your payment is due. Make sure you read all the literature accompanying the application. Late fees can be costly, and several late payments can negatively affect your credit score.

Control Your Spending

Credit cards sometimes tempt people to overspend. Although credit cards are a convenient way to pay for things, and good to have in case

© Ed Fischer/CartoonStock.com

When you use a credit card, it's easy to lose sight of what you're spending, since the money is not being automatically deducted from your bank account. Even small purchases can really add up. When it comes to paying back what you spend, it can be a rude awakening. Make an effort to keep track of your spending so that you reduce financial stress and stay within a realistic budget.

of an emergency, you can quickly get into debt if you spend more than you have. If you can't pay off your credit card in full each month, you have to pay interest on the balance, which means you will pay more for each item you purchase. Credit card debt can quickly spiral out of control, especially if interest continues to accrue each month, making it harder and harder to pay off the credit card balance.

Know When to Put the Card Away

If you can't control your spending and can't pay off your credit card, stop using it. Think about switching to a bank debit card, which draws money directly from your checking account, or a prepaid credit card, which you load with a certain amount of money and can use until the money runs out. Using a prepaid credit card guarantees that you won't spend money you don't have.

Get Help

Be sure to talk to someone if you're having trouble making credit card payments, can't seem to stay within your budget, or feel over-whelmed financially. A financial aid officer, an advisor, a mentor, or someone at the Student Services Center will be able to assist you or can direct you to other helpful campus resources. Managing your finances takes a lot of practice. Don't be afraid to ask questions and get help as soon as you need it.

✔ Credit Card Application Checklist

○ Find a card with no annual fee.

○ Understand how much interest you will be charged if you don't pay the full amount on your credit card each month.

○ Make sure you are not being charged interest on items as soon as you buy them.

○ Understand all fees and penalties for missed or late payments.

Your Credit History

Your credit history is *very* important, both now and in the future. It will influence your ability to borrow money from banks, buy a car, and get a mortgage for a house. Try to avoid negative strikes on your credit history. Pay off your credit cards in full each month; don't waste your money on interest and fees. If you can't afford a certain purchase, wait until you can. Staying in control of your personal finances will significantly reduce your stress and anxiety. And creating a budget will make you more aware of when you should and should not spend money.

How you handle your credit cards has a significant impact on your credit history, so be sure that you fully understand the terms of your credit cards and use them wisely. How you manage your checking account also influences your credit history. For example, if you bounce a check (that is, write a check without sufficient funds in your account), your credit history will be negatively affected. But if you keep close tabs on your spending and write down all purchases and payments, you will be on your way to maintaining a good credit history.

QUICK TIP

Live within Your Means

Strive to live within your means, even if you have to make sacrifices that others don't have to make. Living within your means isn't always easy, but it will help you in the long term, especially if you keep your credit history strong.

Taking the time to understand where you stand financially will be time well spent. And remember, if you need help figuring out how to manage your money, ask someone you trust. It's easy to run into financial trouble. The solution is to immediately address any financial problems so that they don't spiral out of control. Be proactive—you won't regret it.

Q case study

Bill shares his perspective on how to manage finances during college.

I had a work-study job three out of the four years I was in college. In my first year, I didn't have any system for managing my money. That changed when I had to cut back my job hours. I knew I needed to be more careful with my money. I learned more about budgeting by talking to my mentor, and I said no to things that weren't budget friendly. I knew that if I didn't practice budgeting in college, I was going to have a hard time when I entered the working world.

I do have a credit card, but I can use it only for groceries and gas, which is great because I'm not tempted to spend it on clothes or shoes. I have been pretty good at paying it off. However, I do have a balance now that I'm trying to pay off, and I have a plan to commute with a friend twice a week to class and will take the bus into town instead of using my car to reduce my gas expenditures. I also reduced the amount I can spend on personal items I don't really need in my budget until my credit card balance is zero.

QUESTIONS FOR REFLECTION   Have you figured out a budgeting system to keep track of your finances? If so, does it help you keep your credit card payments under control? If not, do you have any attitudes about money that prevent you from putting together a budget?

14

iStock.com/CagriOgner

Staying Healthy and Reducing Stress

S taying healthy and finding ways to reduce stress are important strategies to improve your college experience. Keeping both your mind and your body in good shape will make it easier to manage your college schedule, concentrate in class, study effectively, and perform well on exams. As a college student with many responsibilities and commitments, it can be difficult to find time to exercise, eat well, or get enough sleep. Your many obligations may leave you feeling overwhelmed and stressed. Though it may not seem that way, taking the time to stay healthy will help you be successful throughout college and life. College isn't all work though, and socializing will be an integral part of your college experience. So, it's also important to make sound decisions when engaging in college social life in order to stay healthy and happy during your time in college. The suggestions in this chapter will help you figure out how to balance college life with taking good care of yourself and staying safe.

LaunchPad Solo
macmillan learning

To access the LearningCurve study tool, video activities, and more, go to *LaunchPad Solo for College Success.* macmillanlearning.com/collegesuccessmedia

219

Eat, Sleep, and Exercise

In college, it's important to try to keep your body fueled, to stick to a regular sleep schedule, and to stay physically active. This may seem like simple advice, but staying healthy in college often falls by the wayside when you are coping with a busy schedule, large volumes of work, and exams.

Keep Your Body Fueled

Be sure to make mealtimes a regular part of your routine. Whether you're eating in food courts and dining halls on campus, cooking for yourself, or going out for a meal, be sure to eat food that satisfies you, keeps you energized during class, and fuels your brain while studying and completing assignments. When your brain is working at the high levels required in college, you are expending a lot of energy, and you need enough nourishing fuel to keep you going.

Pick healthy options. Try to eat at least two or three healthy meals a day. What constitutes a "healthy meal"? It's a balanced meal that consists of protein of some sort, carbohydrates (whole-grain foods are best), and lots of fruits and vegetables.

Start the day off right. Every morning, be sure to eat a nutritious breakfast. If you don't have time to prepare something or stop for a bite on campus, keep fruit, nuts, bagels, or cereal readily available. If you tend to sleep through classes or always feel tired, that sluggishness might be a sign that you're not eating anything in the morning. Eating a good breakfast will perk you up.

Stay well fueled all day. Eat snacks between meals. In college, you're always on the go, so be sure to eat a snack that keeps your energy levels up. Grab whatever satisfies you—a banana, a granola bar, a cup of yogurt—and have it ready when you need a pick-me-up.

"I eat vegetables with lots of antioxidants. That's why
I'm still on the first of my nine lives."

© Aaron Bacall/CartoonStock.com

Eating healthy can really make a world of difference to your health. Be
sure to include a lot of vegetables and nutrient-rich food in your diet to
maintain your energy and health during college.

Monitor caffeine intake. Enjoy caffeinated beverages, but find
the right balance. You might feel that you need coffee or soda to
get through the day, but if you overdo it, you might find it difficult
to concentrate. Be aware of how much caffeine you're consuming.
If you consume too much caffeine, you may feel jittery rather than
energized.

Eating well is pretty simple if you make it a priority. Healthy
foods can improve both your energy level and your ability to
concentrate, so be sure to fit in a healthy diet during your college
years.

CHAPTER 14

Visual Walkthrough

Making Balanced Food Choices

In college, you can grab a meal in many places—whether it's the late-night pizza place, the café in the library, or your own refrigerator. Throughout the hustle and bustle of each day, try to choose a variety of healthy foods, with a balance of fruits, vegetables, grains, and protein.

(1) When you're on the go, easy fruit options include apples, bananas, and grapes. And fruit smoothies can be particularly satisfying.

(2) Vegetables might not be your favorite food, but raw carrots are a great snack. Other healthy options include hummus, raw broccoli, celery, asparagus, and zucchini. If you make your own smoothies or shakes, add a handful of spinach or kale.

(3) You can find protein not only in chicken, pork, fish, and beef, but also in eggs, beans, and nuts.

(4) Dairy products are great sources of calcium and protein, so pick up string cheese, add milk to your cereal, and eat a cup of yogurt a day. If you are dairy free, almond milk, soy milk, and rice milk are all good alternatives.

(5) You need good carbohydrates to get you through the day, so grab a granola bar, use whole-grain bread for sandwiches, and eat a healthy cereal in the morning.

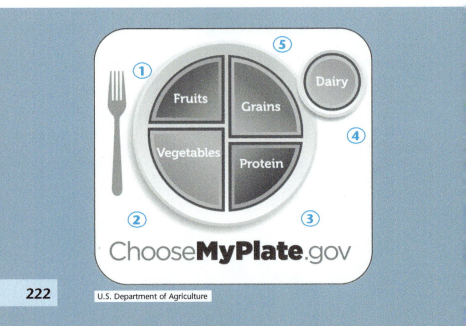

ChooseMyPlate.gov

U.S. Department of Agriculture

QUICK TIP

Talk to Someone

Eating disorders come in many different forms, and can include activities such as overeating, purging, binge eating, or not eating enough. If you think you might have an eating disorder, get help from your mentor, an advisor, or the counseling office. An eating disorder could be a sign that you're struggling with other aspects of college life, so be sure to ask for help.

Find a Sleep Solution

In college, some students find that they're sleeping more than ever because they don't have morning classes. Other students may sleep less than normal because they are juggling so many things. Yet others experience shifts in their sleep schedules—sometimes they stay up all night and then sleep during the day. Whatever your sleep preferences, take some time when you begin college to figure out a sleep pattern that works best for you.

Sleep—or lack of sleep—can have a significant impact on your energy level and your ability to concentrate. Are you most productive when you stay up late to study and complete assignments? If so, can you still stay attentive in class? Or do you find that you can't even stay awake during the lecture? Do you prefer to go to sleep and wake up early to get work done before classes start? If you can, schedule your classes in a way that capitalizes on your energy levels. For instance, if you are more energized in the morning, it may be better to take earlier classes. If you always get tired in the early afternoon, a class at that time might not be the best decision; instead schedule something that requires less energy and focus.

Try to find a sleep schedule that makes you feel productive and energized. You may not be able to get eight hours of sleep a night, but try to sleep at least six or seven hours. Maybe an afternoon nap will fill the sleep deficit. Occasionally, you may get less sleep than the ideal amount for you—for example, the night before a test or when a paper is due. But as soon as you can, try to get back to a regular sleep pattern.

⑤ Questions to Ask Yourself If You're Struggling to Get Enough Sleep

1. Am I engaged in too many obligations outside of academics?

Consider how many hours you need to dedicate to academics, your other obligations such as work and family, and sleep, then think carefully about what else you can realistically fit into your schedule.

2. Am I taking too many credits?

It can be tempting to take more than the suggested number of classes or credit hours during a term for various reasons. There are times when this may be necessary, but not if your sleep is negatively impacted. If you're not staying rested, you won't be able to think and perform as well as you could.

3. Should I try to reduce or shift my job hours if possible?

If you have a job and find that it's very difficult to balance your hours with getting enough sleep, see if you're able to reduce your hours, and if that's not possible, consider shifting your hours to different days or different parts of the day to try to improve your sleep patterns.

4. Have I noticed myself procrastinating before starting my course work?

Procrastination often leads to less sleep. When time needed to work on assignments and study for tests is wasted, sleep is sacrificed since the work ultimately needs to get done. Try hard to work on time management skills that reduce your tendency to procrastinate so you can get your work done and get to sleep!

5. Am I struggling in my classes?

If you notice that you're staying up very late spending a lot of time trying to understand class material and complete assignments, you may be in a class or classes that are challenging or possibly too difficult. Get help from your instructor, a mentor, an advisor, or an academic support office on campus to try to help you manage the course load.

Exercise Can Make All the Difference

One thing that can enhance your well-being in college is exercise. Physical activity of all kinds relieves tension and stress, provides more oxygen to your body, and gives your active brain a much-needed break. You don't have to go to the gym seven days a week to get the benefits of exercise. Once you find a physical activity that you enjoy, engage in it four or five times a week. You'll feel better—and you'll perform better in college.

 Ways to Fit Exercise into a Busy College Schedule

1. **Instead of taking the shuttle or driving, walk to your farthest class.**

   This strategy is an easy way to fit in some regular exercise if you're struggling to find the time for physical activity.

2. **Use a bike as your mode of transportation.**

   This is another great way to fit exercise into a busy schedule. And if you bike, you might even get to class and other commitments faster than if you take a shuttle or a car.

3. **Attend a scheduled class at the gym, such as yoga or kickboxing, to motivate you.**

   Put the class in your planner so that you remember to go. And if the class is more fun than other types of exercise, you will have an extra incentive to get to the gym.

4. **Participate in an activity, such as a running group, to combine your interests with meaningful exercise.**

   You need to find a balance in college, so try combining your social life with physical activity. Participate in a group activity that not only appeals to you but also provides the added bonus of some exercise.

5. **Join a sports team that is fun.**

   Most college campuses offer many athletic opportunities—both competitive and noncompetitive. Also look for local sports teams in your town or city. Joining a sports team is a way to get some exercise as well as to bond with others.

Manage Your Stress

Stress is a fact of life in college, especially during your first year when everything is new. You may experience stress for many different reasons. Maybe you're away from home for the first time or are trying to balance college classes with a demanding job and family life. Perhaps you don't understand material in certain classes and are struggling to choose your major. Given that you will undoubtedly experience some stress in college, you need to be able to manage it effectively.

Build a Community

It is important to build a community of people on campus you trust. Find instructors, mentors, advisors, or other campus staff you can talk to about the ups and downs of your college experience so that they can assist you. Seek out students whom you feel you can connect to. It takes time to build true friendships, but if you make the effort to connect with other students with similar interests, you will begin to build your own community. Participate in events that bring together people from your culture, religion, or ethnicity. Take the initiative in building a support system that is there when you need it.

Stay Connected

It may take a while to find support on campus; until you do, manage your stress by staying in touch with family, friends, and mentors from your pre-college life. If you're struggling with classes and haven't yet found someone on campus to talk to, think about any former teachers, administrators, or mentors you could call on or reach out to. When you need to talk to someone who really understands you, call your best friend, partner, or a family member. We all derive strength and hope from others, so reach out to someone when you need to. Staying connected is essential for your mental health.

"They've all tested positive for stress."

Most college students experience varying amounts of stress throughout college. Try a few different ways to reduce stress to see what works for you. And remember that you're not alone—you can get help from campus resources such as the counseling center whenever you need help managing your stress.

Be Good to Yourself

To alleviate anxiety and tension and maintain a sense of calm, incorporate the following suggestions into your lifestyle.

Stay healthy. The more you maintain a healthy lifestyle, the more you can reduce your stress levels. Eat nutritious foods that you enjoy; take a nap, if it will help you make it through the day; go to the gym; or get some exercise outdoors. Physical activity can melt away stress, at least for a short time. If stress is making you anxious and short of breath, physical activity will help you breathe more easily. Even tensing and relaxing muscles while at your computer can help.

Stay organized. Disorganization can cause unnecessary stress. If you're always late to meetings because you forget to write them down in your planner or if you keep losing class syllabi because you stick them in a messy pile of papers on your desk, you're adding stress to your life. If you start practicing time management strategies, you'll be able to stay organized and to keep track of your schedule, course requirements, and commitments.

Take breaks. In college, you're always on the go and might forget to take some time to relax. No matter whether you're engaged in a marathon study session, writing a ten-page paper, in the midst of rehearsing for an upcoming performance, or working on a challenging project at your job, you need to take an occasional break and recharge your batteries. Go outside in the fresh air. Enjoy a snack. Listen to your favorite music. Call a friend. Read a book for enjoyment. Watch your favorite TV show.

Do something brainless. When you work your brain too much, you can become stressed and tired. Do something that doesn't require you to think for a while. Do some spring cleaning, listen to your favorite music, go to a movie, or check Facebook.

Rest and relax. On weekends, give yourself permission to take a long break. Whether you escape for a few hours or for the whole afternoon, make time for true rest and relaxation. Take a hike or go on a short road trip. Meet friends for coffee and a movie. Take your family to a museum or the park. It doesn't matter what the activity is; just be sure that it leaves you feeling rested and relaxed.

Engage in activities you enjoy. Don't participate in activities that just add more stress to your life. Instead, engage in activities and organizations that you love. Be sure to choose what *you* want to do, not what your friends are doing or what you think will build your résumé. Time is precious in college, and the time you spend outside of class and work should leave you feeling invigorated, not drained.

Reward yourself. Be sure to recognize your hard work in college, even if your grades don't always reflect your intellect and abilities. If you're putting your best effort into classes, papers, and studying, pat yourself on the back once in a while. College is a time of great personal growth. Reflect on how far you've come, the challenges you're facing, and how much you're doing and learning. Be good to yourself—give yourself some sort of reward, whether it's an ice cream sundae or a concert on campus.

Get help from campus resources. If you're feeling over-whelmed by stress, ask yourself why. Then decide whether your mentor or someone else on the campus staff might be able to help you find techniques for relieving the stress. Remember, you're never alone.

✔ Checklist for Staying Healthy

- ⭘ Eat regularly, and choose healthy, balanced food options whenever possible.
- ⭘ Make sleep a priority so that you get at least six or seven hours of sleep a night.
- ⭘ Find physical activities that make you feel rejuvenated, and exercise regularly.
- ⭘ Keep yourself organized to reduce unnecessary stress.
- ⭘ Take breaks regularly so that your brain and body can rest and relax.
- ⭘ Make time for activities that are fun and meaningful.
- ⭘ Be kind to yourself, and find ways to reward yourself when you deserve recognition.
- ⭘ Get help from campus resources if you're stressed or need to talk to someone about issues with eating, sleep, or exercise.

Q case study

Alicia explains how she learned to manage her stress.

In college, my health suffered as a result of my stress levels. I experienced difficulty concentrating and suffered from anxiety that made it hard to sleep and eat. When my grades and friendships started to suffer, I realized I needed to find a way to manage my stress. Even though it was scary, I talked with my mentor about what I was going through. With support from my mentor and a few others, I decided to join a theater group and a dance team. I also started taking advantage of the health center on my campus and committed to weekly visits. I participated in a paid blogging-for-college opportunity that allowed me to share my college experience in a more positive light. I taught other students how to dance. I started to live for myself and to do things that brought joy into my life.

As a first-year college student, it is important to understand what you can do to manage the stress you will experience. I tried a variety of activities and recognized that if something doesn't work, try again; if it still doesn't work, try something new. People say that it's important to find your niche in college, and when I did, I found that I was better able to deal with stress that came my way.

QUESTIONS FOR REFLECTION   Have you found effective ways to manage the stress you've experienced in college? If so, what makes the biggest impact on reducing your stress? If you haven't yet found effective ways of dealing with stress, have you asked a mentor or an advisor for help?

Be Safe Socially

For the most part, being social in college allows you to connect with others, have fun, and relieve stress. However, some social situations are likely to involve alcohol or even drugs. And some social situations may be out of your control. Staying safe involves pre-planning, knowing yourself, communicating clearly, and seeking help when necessary.

Substance Abuse

Alcohol and drug abuse are serious problems on many college campuses. In college, you'll likely be in social situations where drugs and alcohol are present, giving you access to these substances maybe for the first time. Irresponsible use of these substances can have a negative impact on your college experience and your future. If you choose to engage in drug and alcohol use during college, it's important to have a safety plan in place that honors your limits.

Alcohol. In social situations that include alcohol, think about how you want to handle the situation before entering the social setting. This will give you time to figure out who will be going with you and how you plan to have fun while ensuring that your health and safety are your top priority.

It's also important to know your own limits with alcohol. Always be aware of how much and how fast you are drinking and stay aware of what's going on around you.

It's important to always have at least one friend with you when you go out. Agree to stop drinking or to go home together if one of you has hit a limit or whenever you feel out of control or over-whelmed. And be sure to call for a cab, Uber, or campus transportation service (that are often free to students) if you have had too much to drink.

QUICK TIP

Recognize the Patterns of Binge Drinking

Binge drinking elevates blood alcohol concentrations very quickly—generally after four drinks for women and five drinks for men in a span of just two hours.[1] Binge drinking is often associated with alcohol problems, including alcohol abuse and dependence, alcohol poisoning, injury, and even death. Reaching out for help may be scary, but it could save your future and even your life. You don't have to suffer alone. If you think you fit the pattern of binge drinking, talk to someone at the student support center, counseling office, or health center.

Drugs. Like drinking, illicit drugs can also be a part of college social situations. And like drinking, doing drugs is both dangerous and risky. Depending on the type of drug, illicit drugs can produce side effects such as drowsiness, disorientation, increased heart rate, delusions, and hallucinations. A drug overdose can lead to convulsions, coma, or even death. And because almost 13 percent of young people eighteen to twenty-five drive while under the influence of illicit drugs, there are serious risks to others.[2]

Use of illegal drugs can also lead to drug addiction, which is a compulsive need to use drugs on a regular basis in order to function normally. Addiction is a serious disease that can cause problems in all aspects of your life—harming your relationships, academics, work life, and health. Watch for the signs of addiction, such as neglecting your responsibilities as a student and at work, fighting more than normal, engaging in risky behavior, and avoiding activities you used to enjoy.[3] Seek help. If you find that your life revolves around drugs, even though you know they are hurting you, seek help. Staff at your college's counseling office, health clinic, or student support center want to help. If friends or others you trust on campus reach out and urge you to get help, listen to them. They have your best interests at heart.

---

[1]National Institute on Alcohol Abuse and Alcoholism (NIAAA), April 2012, 1.

[2]US Department of Health and Human Services, 2010 National Survey on Drug Use and Health Results.

[3]Ibid., "Symptoms."

Consequences. Drinking to excess or abusing drugs can have negative ramifications for you and your future. Your academic life will suffer if drinking or drugs become a significant focus of your time. And beyond academic consequences, there are potential legal risks as well. Possession of illegal drugs or underage drinking can lead to probation, expulsion, and arrest. If you decide to take risks, be sure you understand the consequences you might face. Although you may feel invincible in college, you can make one big mistake that could have a significant impact on your future.

Protecting Yourself against Sexual Assault

Sexual assault is a serious problem on many college campuses. Although sexual assault can happen to anybody, the majority of the victims are women, many of whom are attacked by somebody they know, whether a date or an acquaintance. And most victims will not report the crime. An estimated 97,000 students between the ages of eighteen and twenty-four are victims of alcohol-related sexual assault or date rape each year.[4] The following provides some advice on how to best protect yourself and others:

- Go to social gatherings with friends. Make a pact to watch out for each other through the course of the night and leave together.

- Trust your intuition.

- Stay aware and alert. If you are drinking, be aware of how much alcohol you are consuming.

- Whether you're on a date or meet someone at a party, be clear about your expectations when it comes to sexual activity. Try not to be alone with people you don't know very well.

- If you are drinking alcohol, make sure you make or pour your own drink and keep it in view at all times. If you put the drink down for a while, don't hesitate to get a new one.

- Look out for your friends; if you understand what to do in an emergency and how to get help when necessary, you'll be helping those you care about most.

---

[4] NIAAA, April 2012, 1.

If you find yourself in a situation where you feel powerless to stop what's happening or you have been raped, try to get help immediately. Many schools have sexual assault offices with twenty-four-hour hotlines staffed by trained counselors who are ready to help. Program that hotline number—as well as the numbers of the campus police and college health clinic—into your cell phone. When you call the hotline, a counselor will help you figure out where to go and what to do. If your school does not have a hotline, you can seek out help at a local rape crisis center, the police department, student health center, local emergency room, or speak with a campus chaplain. To obtain the support and assistance you need, it is very helpful to talk to a trained professional immediately.

Although the topic of sexual assault isn't an easy one, it's important to address this issue so that you can better protect yourself and others. Know that you aren't alone. And don't keep silent if you are a victim of sexual assault.

Consider Your Safety Online

The Internet is an integral part of social life for most of us, especially students, but, sadly, the Internet isn't always a friendly place. Given the number of people who can access the information you post to social media sites, you can't possibly know the intentions of every person who views your photos, status updates, and personal information. Be careful when you post personal information online. You may think that only friends and family can view your information, but that may not be the case. Your privacy settings won't always protect you, so assume that almost anyone can and will see what you've posted. For example, if you allow friends of friends to view the information on your Facebook page, you don't really know who those "friends of friends" might be.

On the Internet, it is easy to find and exchange information. If you ever feel as though your safety is at risk—if you have received offensive, violent, or abusive messages, or if you feel that someone you are connected to online is crossing boundaries—talk immediately to an instructor, a mentor, a college staff member, or a security person at your college. A boundary violation can be something as simple as posting a picture with a label or texting in a way that just doesn't feel right. Don't ignore your gut feeling, because your gut is usually right.

15

iStock.com/CagriOgner

Starting Your Career Journey

A lot happens in your first year of college. You meet classmates, learn about campus resources, get to know your instructors, choose a mentor, figure out an academic plan, hone college study skills, engage in social life, and manage your money. And as you move through your remaining years of college, you'll have even more to think about, including your career interests and possible jobs you might want to pursue after graduation. Even if you already have a job or a chosen career, college gives you the opportunity to reflect on your career path and to build the skills necessary to obtain employment and succeed in your career. The more thought, exploration, and preparation you put into your career options now, the more closely your progress through college will reflect your career goals and interests. It's important to figure out what college experiences—academic and nonacademic—you should engage in and reflect on to confirm any career interests you already have or to help you determine what careers you're really interested in exploring.

LaunchPad Solo
macmillan learning

To access the LearningCurve study tool, video activities, and more, go to *LaunchPad Solo for College Success.* macmillanlearning.com/collegesuccessmedia

Dig into Your Interests

Ideally, the career path you choose will involve something you're interested in. And while it may not be possible to find a job that perfectly fits your interests, focusing on your academic interests and your preferences outside the classroom will give you a great deal of insight into what you like to do and how you like to spend your time. Reflecting deeply on your interests and preferences provides essential data about yourself as you begin thinking about potential careers.

Narrow Down Your Career Choices

Selecting a career is a highly personal endeavor. Your career path will be unique to you, and you have control in shaping it. And while your skills matter significantly as you consider future jobs and careers, also take the time to carefully consider your personal preferences. You'll want to find jobs and a career path that are not only a good fit in terms of your skills, but a good fit in terms of your interests. College is a great time to consider your preferences, since you have to work very hard academically, may also have a job, and could be engaged outside the classroom in activities or organizations. This exposure to many different types of experiences will help you narrow down the best career fit and environments for you.

Start by considering what type of academic work is most interesting to you and any work you do outside the classroom. Do you enjoy being creative, solving problems, or analyzing data? Do you feel personally fulfilled when you are working for a particular cause? Similarly, begin noticing when you are particularly engaged in what you are doing. Is there a specific type of class that has really captured your interest, or maybe a specific type of assignment you have enjoyed completing in the past? Is there a project for your job or volunteer position that is keeping you focused and excited? Seeing what you like and dislike about your work experiences is the first step in figuring out what's most important to you.

⑤ Questions to Ask When Identifying Your Career Preferences

1. What academic work do I find most engaging and why?

By writing down the academic topics you are most engaged in and the assignments that are most engrossing, you gain important insight into your interests and your work preferences.

2. How do I feel about working in groups vs. working alone?

Determining what work style fits you best can help you determine what career fields may be a better fit—and if you don't have a strong preference for either, that is helpful information, too.

3. What activities are my favorites and why?

Activities you engage in may reveal hidden passions that could help you focus on specific careers that are related in some way. The way you spend your time outside of class can reveal interests that you may be able to connect to your future career.

4. What type of work environment do I want to work in?

Do you want to be a part of a start-up or a more established organization? What values do you want your employer to have? Do you want to work in an office, at home, or outdoors? Figuring out a good career fit involves figuring out the environment you would best fit into.

5. What first comes to mind when I hear the question "What are my values?"

Take time to consider the values you hold dear so that the careers you consider incorporate what matters to you.

QUICK TIP

Keep an Open Mind

You may surprise yourself and fall in love with a career you never imagined. Or maybe you'll find that your strengths are better suited for another career. Be open to new career possibilities as you reflect on your interests, your preferences, and your academic successes and challenges.

Connect Your Academic Plan to Your Career

Take time to periodically step back and reflect on your academic plan and major in relation to your career interests. Maybe you've chosen a major that sets you on a specific career path, or maybe your academic plan involves many classes you love, but you're still uncertain about what career you'll pursue after you graduate. Both scenarios are normal, and both require constant critical thinking about what is working and what is not working for you academically.

Look for patterns in your academic plan that point to career interests. Notice any class patterns that begin developing in your academic plan. Figure out why you have decided to take certain classes and whether they speak to any future career interests. Similarly, look at classes that you haven't enjoyed and use that feedback to eliminate any careers you are currently considering that might not be a good fit.

Adjust your academic plan according to your career goals. Use your time in college to test your career interests through adjusting your academic plan. For example, if you're focused on a career in business, but aren't sure what aspect of business you're most interested in, add business classes to your academic plan that give you exposure to different fields in business, such as accounting or marketing.

Be mindful that some career paths require additional schooling. It's important to learn about any courses you need to incorporate into your academic plan if you want to apply for higher levels of education to enable you to consider or pursue a specific career. Even if you're not sure about the career field, it doesn't hurt to be prepared in this way so that if you do want to apply, you won't lack the necessary requirements.

Get Experience

There are many opportunities in college, beyond academics, that will help you gain experience and test your skills and interests. And there are also concrete steps you can take that will not only give you insight into career paths you might want to consider, but will improve your chances of finding positions and open up doors within the career fields you're interested in pursuing.

Exploring Your Options

Consider the many ways that you're able to explore jobs and career options during college. You might want to explore internship and shadowing opportunities, volunteer, perform research, attend guests lectures and conferences, run for leadership roles in student organizations, find an on- or off-campus job, and use any resources you might have at your career office.

Internship and shadowing experiences are a window into the career. If you're able to spend time working with or observing aspects of the job or career field, you'll have a better gauge of what you like and don't like, providing important information as you consider your career options.

Volunteer opportunities can be meaningful and helpful. Volunteering is a great way to give back and to gain experience working for something that matters to you. Consider what aspects of the volunteer position you enjoy the most and why you're volunteering in the first place.

Research positions provide an opportunity to assist on an important project. Pursuing research you're interested in is like trying out a job where you may have to do tasks that are a bit mundane, but they are essential as you work toward a higher purpose related to the ultimate goal of the research. Figure out what you do and don't like about engaging in research and how it might inform your thinking about future careers.

Attending guest lectures and conferences opens up learning opportunities. Hearing experts speak about their experiences is a great way to gain knowledge and provides the chance to ask any questions you might have. Similarly, engaging in a conference allows you to focus on a specific topic in depth with others who are interested and invested.

Leadership roles in student organizations may reveal your passions and values. If you plan to take on a leadership role, it's usually in an organization that really means something to you. Take time to think about why you took on the leadership position, what you are getting out of it, and how it can help you think about career prospects.

On- or off-campus jobs are a great way to look at your skill set. Any kind of work experience will help you figure out what your strengths and weaknesses are, what you might want to improve, what type of work environment suits or doesn't suit you, and what type of work you might prefer if you have the opportunity.

Use career services resources whenever you can. Figure out what career services are available on your campus. If possible, utilize these services to connect with career counselors to discuss all aspects of your career search, attend career panels, use online resources to help with résumés and cover letters, and to connect with alumni in different career fields. Finding support and gaining valuable career insight can only help you as you look for jobs and figure out your career path.

✓ Checklist of College Opportunities to Consider

- ○ Internship and shadowing opportunities that give you experience
- ○ Volunteer opportunities that could be particularly meaningful
- ○ Research experiences on or off campus
- ○ Attending guest lectures or conferences about exciting topics
- ○ Leading a campus organization you're passionate about
- ○ On- or off-campus jobs to get real-world experience
- ○ Use of career services

Connecting with Others

As you gain experience in college to help you think more critically about your interests, preferences, skills, passions, and values in relation to potential future careers, there are additional steps you can take to get started on your career journey. You'll want to find ways to learn more deeply about specific jobs and careers and to connect with others in specific fields, while also preparing yourself for these important interactions.

Arrange informational interviews. An informational interview is a wonderful way to gain insight into jobs in your career field. Ask a career counselor, a mentor, family members, or experienced students for the names of people who have the types of jobs that are of interest to you. Then, contact these people, and ask to talk with them for a short while about the nature of their job. People usually enjoy talking about their careers, especially if you are seeking information rather than explicitly asking them for a job.

Cultivate a professional identity online. As you begin to explore your career options, remember that the Internet is a powerful way to both put yourself out there for the world to see and to connect to others in career fields of interest. Be sure to present a professional, mature, and positive appearance online. Basically, be smart about what you post. Remember, the words you type and the pictures you post online are easy to share with others and difficult to delete. Assume that anyone—including employers and college officials—can see what's on your Facebook profile, for example. Do you really want the pictures you just posted to be seen by the company that interviewed you for the summer internship of your dreams? Your reputation, college status, job opportunities, and admission to graduate school are on the line, so remember: nothing is completely private online.

Start networking. During college, you should begin practicing the important skill of networking, or the art of making connections with others. Networking with professionals in different careers—whether through internships you've had, informational interviews you've

⑤ **Ways** to Make the Most of Informational Interviews

1. **Research the career field, the job, and the interviewer.**

Any preliminary research you can do will give you a general sense of the career field, allowing you to gain a more in-depth perspective on the job. You won't waste time on the basics, and you'll have a sense of the person's background as a good point of reference.

2. **Prepare at least five or more questions ahead of time.**

You need to lead the informational interview and are expected to be the one to ask questions, so preparing ahead of time will ensure you feel as comfortable as possible and get the most out of the meeting.

3. **Think about why you are interested in the field and be prepared to talk about it.**

The person you are meeting with will want to understand why you scheduled the meeting, so sharing why you are interested in the field is key to making a connection.

4. **Take notes.**

It's helpful to take notes on salient aspects of the conversation that you might want to reflect on later or in case you have follow-up questions.

5. **Send a thank-you note and keep in touch.**

Always send a thank-you note that shares what you got out of the informational interview and let the person who interviewed you know that you'll plan to keep him or her updated on your career journey.

conducted, or alumni you've reached out to—not only will help you learn more but can also give you an advantage if jobs become available. People in your network will often remember your interest in a career field or position and want to be helpful. They might tell you about an available job opening or put in a good word if you've already applied. Networking really can open up doors.

Work on your résumé and cover letter. When you apply for summer positions, internships, and jobs after graduation, you'll need to submit a résumé and a cover letter. For help in preparing these two documents, meet with a career counselor, a mentor or advisor, or someone you trust to be sure you have included all the necessary information, formatted the documents properly, and caught any grammatical or spelling errors. A résumé is essentially a summary of your educational background, work experience, and outside activities and interests, while your cover letter is your chance to "speak" directly to the employer about why you are applying for the position and what makes you a good fit for the job. Remember: your résumé and cover letter will be the first impression potential employers have of you.

© Fran/CartoonStock.com

Potential employers will notice errors on written correspondence, no matter how trivial. Take the time to thoroughly edit and proofread everything you send so that employers will focus on your experience and skills, not on careless mistakes.

Visual Walkthrough

Résumé Writing

Your résumé provides an overview of your skills, accomplishments, experience, and interests. It takes some effort to put together a résumé that employers will notice. Be sure to take the time necessary to create a résumé that is thorough, easy to read, concise, organized, interesting, and accurate, and think carefully about ways to highlight your strengths. And remember to use the counselors at the Career Services Office—they can help you determine what information to include in your résumé and can also offer feedback on what changes might improve your résumé.

(1) Include your contact information on your résumé so that potential employers know how to reach you.

(2) Put your education information at the top of your résumé, and add important academic details to highlight your academic interests and accomplishments.

(3) Include sections that describe your work and volunteer experience, as well as any significant activities, in order to give employers an idea of your skills, expertise, and interests.

(4) Include dates on your résumé because employers want to know when your experiences took place and how long you engaged in them. List items in reverse chronological order, putting your most recent experiences at the top of each section.

(5) Add succinct details about your experience and activities to demonstrate your accomplishments, responsibilities, skills, and leadership abilities.

(6) To create a fuller picture of yourself, add a section that highlights your skills and interests.

Kevin Nathans

1-555-321-1234 • E-mail: kevin.nathans@email.com

123 Main Street, East Lansing, MI 42524

EDUCATION

Michigan State University (MSU), College of Engineering
East Lansing, MI   Expect to graduate May 2019
B.A. in Computer Science and Engineering. Additional course work in Economics and Spanish.

Farmington High School, Farmington, MI   Graduated June 2015
Achievements: National Honor Society, Senior Class Treasurer, Science Honor Society President, Soccer Team Captain.

WORK/VOLUNTEER EXPERIENCE

Department of Computer Science and Engineering, MSU,
East Lansing, MI   September 2016–Present
Research Assistant in Games for Entertainment and Learning Lab
- Devote 6–8 hours a week to research focused on innovative and educational digital games.
- Train in research methods and 3-D computer science gaming methods.

State Farm Insurance, Livonia, MI   Summer 2016
Claims Assistant
- Responded to inquiries about the status of insurance claims and worked closely with managers to process claims.
- Reorganized computer system in office to increase efficiency and improve electronic communication.

MSU Alternative Spring Break, New Orleans, LA   March 2016
Team Leader
- Organized Habitat for Humanity volunteer experience for 30 participants as an alternative spring break option.
- Led a team of 10 on-site in New Orleans and completed the paint job throughout the two-story house.

ACTIVITIES

MSU Student Engineering Council, East Lansing, MI   November 2016–Present
Treasurer
- Oversee funds for campus events and help organize yearly conferences for the Michigan engineering community.

MSU Ultimate Frisbee Club Team, East Lansing, MI   September 2015–Present
Co-captain
- Run practices for teammates, schedule competition with other colleges, play in games regularly.

MSU Student Government Academic Assembly,
East Lansing, MI   September 2015–May 2016
First-Year Representative
- Contributed to meetings focused on academic policies and tuition issues. Communicated any changes to first-year classmates.

SKILLS & INTERESTS

- Languages: Spanish (fluent), French (proficient).
- Computer Skills: Advanced programming in C++, experience with Excel and PowerPoint.
- Interests: Hiking, soccer, tennis, skiing, playing piano, computer gaming.

Visual Walkthrough, continued

Cover Letter

A cover letter is an important document, since it can either help or hurt your chances of getting the job you're applying for. In just a few paragraphs you need to explain succinctly why you're interested in the position and why you have the skills and potential to be successful in the role. It takes time to write a solid cover letter, as well as a lot of editing, and you should get someone you trust to review your letter before you submit it.

1. Recognize that the structure of a cover letter should always include your contact information, the date of the letter, and the contact information of the person you are writing to.

2. Be sure to include a salutation, or a greeting that is appropriate, depending on the person or group you are writing to. For example, when writing a formal cover letter, use "Dear" and any titles that are necessary such as Professor, President, Mr., Mrs., Ms., Sir/Madam, and so on. When writing to a group, you may want to address the letter to "Members of the Committee," or "To whom it may concern."

3. Start the letter by clearly and briefly stating what you are applying for and why you are interested in and qualified for the position.

4. Illustrate, using recent examples and specific details, how your experience fits with the position, why you would be a good fit, and what you could contribute.

5. If it makes sense, express an interest in meeting or calling to further demonstrate your interest in the position, and always offer a word of thanks at the end of the letter.

Kevin Nathans

123 Main Street
East Lansing, MI 42524
1-555-321-1234
kevin.nathans@email.com

January 8, 2017

Professor Timothy Bodell
Computer Science and Engineering Department
Michigan State University
3115 Engineering Building
428 S. Shaw Lane
East Lansing, MI 48824

Dear Professor Bodell,

I would like to apply for the Software Engineering Internship in the Computer Science and Engineering Department at MSU. As a sophomore majoring in Computer Science and Engineering, I have realized my deep interest in software development and believe this opportunity would allow me to draw on my recent experience and further explore the ins and outs of this important area of computer science.

My experience as a Research Assistant in the Games for Entertainment and Learning Lab has prepared me for this internship because I have had the chance to shadow and support professors and graduate students while they have been developing new software to enhance the capabilities of educational digital games. I also will participate in a project focused on 3-D computer science gaming methods during the upcoming spring semester that will further my understanding of how software can be used to innovate in this area.

Being involved in MSU's Student Engineering Council as Treasurer has also been a valuable experience as I have had the opportunity to meet many other peers and upperclassmen with a passion for software engineering. I believe my passion, along with the dedication I have given to my course work, would allow me to contribute to the Computer Science and Engineering Department if I was able to work as an intern and would also expand my skills in significant ways.

I would be happy to meet with you or set up a call to discuss my background and interest in more detail. Thank you in advance for your consideration.

Sincerely,
Kevin Nathans

Engage in mock interviews. Once you send out your résumé and cover letter, an employer might ask you to engage in an online, phone, or in-person interview. Practicing for interviews will put you more at ease during the actual interview. Find out if your career office provides opportunities to engage in mock interviews or set up an appointment with a college staff member you know and practice answering potential interview questions. Working with another person who is able to give you honest feedback about your interview skills will help you understand what is important to convey to employers during an interview and how you can best highlight your strengths and interest in the position.

Don't Hesitate to Get Help

Figuring out your future and getting relevant work experience can sometimes be an overwhelming task. During your journey, seek out the help of others. If you have a career services office at your college, career counselors or trained staff can help you make decisions about your future career. And having career-focused conversations with a mentor, an advisor, an experienced student, or your peers is also incredibly useful because talking with others helps you articulate what may be spinning in your head and can help you organize your thoughts. These career conversations can help you evaluate career paths available to you and the many job possibilities within those careers. With guidance, you can think more carefully and critically about relevant factors that could influence your career and job decisions.

Another important group to connect with for career advice are college alumni who can provide insight into career fields they have pursued and may be able to help you with job searches in those fields. If your college has a list of alumni willing to speak to college students, take advantage of this resource. Your college might also offer recruiting opportunities during which employers come to the campus to meet with students at a job fair. These employers usually have open positions students can apply for. Find out when your campus will be hosting a job fair and how to engage in the process.

© Fran/CartoonStock.com

Are you feeling stuck? Career planning can take a lot of work, and it can be an overwhelming process at times just figuring out how to get from "here to there." Just know that you aren't alone. Reach out to your college supports for guidance and encouragement.

QUICK TIP

Tap into Online Resources

In addition to connecting with others in person, search online for advice on preparing résumés and cover letters, conducting informational interviews, searching for jobs, and interviewing with potential employers. There is a wealth of information out there at your disposal, and most of it is free!

Q case study

Sasha explains how she explored her career interests in college.

After my first year, I wanted to know what careers were available to someone with a degree in economics and what steps I needed to take to do well as an economics major. Along the way, I learned some valuable lessons that helped me better understand my passions and goals.

1. *Take advantage of the resources on campus.* My college's Career Services Office is the best place on campus to help you figure out what you want to do with your life and how to accomplish your career goals. The office is staffed by professionals who are trained to assist college students with career-related issues. It's also a good place to meet other students who share your concerns.

2. *Pursue activities that interest you.* While I was in college, I joined the Business Club and volunteered at the local newspaper. I met upperclassmen who majored in economics and could help guide me in the right direction. Not only was I able to share my thoughts openly and comfortably, but I also built great relationships.

3. *Try to secure a summer internship in the fall or early spring.* It is important to start looking into summer internships as early as you can. Your internship does not need to be a paid position, but it should relate to your interests.

4. *Network on and off campus.* Networking involves much more than handing out résumés or business cards and asking for jobs or leads. To be effective at networking, you must show a genuine interest in the other person, build a strong rapport by being friendly and enthusiastic, and recognize that networking is a two-way process in which you share information and advice.

5. *Seek out programs that can help you with internships and career development.* Most of these programs can be found at the Career Services Office. In my first year, I applied for the INROADS program, which is a rigorous career-development program designed for students with an interest in fields such as business, finance, IT, communications, and human resources.

I used a number of resources to help me explore my career interests. My summer internships were the most helpful. After my first year in college, I knew that I had an interest in finance, but I didn't know exactly what I wanted to do in that field. My internships helped shape my interest and passion. I kept a journal about my experiences; I shared my experiences and constantly sought advice.

QUESTIONS FOR REFLECTION   Have you explored what career services your college offers? If so, what have you found to be most valuable, and why? If not, consider making an appointment with a career counselor or advisor to learn about the extensive resources available and talking with a professional about your interests, passions, and goals.

Dealing with the Unexpected

Searching for a job is never easy and is often stressful, especially when the economy is bad. If you graduate from college at a time when jobs are scarce, you may have to look for jobs in areas outside your preferred career field. And finding a job may take you much longer than you had hoped.

Remember that you're never alone as you search for a job. Take full advantage of the career services office (if you have one), alumni resources on your college campus, and the contacts you've made during your time in school, such as mentors, advisors, instructors, staff, or past employers. Although they might not be able to speed up the job search process, they can provide you with support and advice as you face these difficulties.

It's Your Life

College is a time for academic and personal exploration and growth. When you graduate, you will not be the same person you were when you entered as a first-year student. The opportunities that present themselves throughout college will help shape you. Although you won't be able to do everything at the same time, especially as you work on finding a balance in college, figure out what opportunities you don't want to miss, and make sure to build them into your overall college and future plans.

Notice What Matters to You

By embracing all that college has to offer and by noticing what you find most interesting, you'll be on your way to better understanding who you are and what you want for your future. There is so much to learn in college, and your greatest insights will sometimes come from the most unexpected places. For example, you may volunteer regularly and soon realize that you want a career that connects in some way to the cause you're so passionate about. Or studying abroad may open your eyes to global possibilities and lead you to consider jobs in foreign countries.

You will be very busy in college, but try to pause periodically to take in all that you're experiencing and all that you're learning. Self-reflection will help you make the most of college and will allow you to consider what's really important to you. Also, remember the value of talking with and learning from others. When you reach out to others—whether it's for coffee with a mentor or for extra help in a class—you will gain a wealth of knowledge, support, and insight. Reach out, make connections, and be true to yourself. College is a time to get to know yourself. Make the most of it!

Index

"5 Questions" Lists

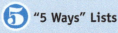 **"5 Ways" Lists**

case studies

 **Checklists**

Getting Started Guides

QUICK TIPS

Visual Walkthroughs

Note: This custom edition of *A Pocket Guide to College Success*, Second Edition, for Laramie County Community College omits Chapter 11, Chapter 13, Appendix A, and Appendix B, which are not covered by your instructors. As a result, you will find gaps in pagination that are intentional.

Contents